of the IMITATION of CHRIST

of the IMITATION *of* CHRIST

THOMAS À KEMPIS

Whitaker House

All Scripture quotations are taken from the King James Version of the Bible.

Editor's note: This book has been edited for the modern reader. Words, expressions, and sentence structure have been updated for clarity and readability.

OF THE IMITATION OF CHRIST

ISBN: 0-88368-952-9
Printed in the United States of America
© 1981 by Whitaker House

Whitaker House
30 Hunt Valley Circle
New Kensington, PA 15068
website: www.whitakerhouse.com

CONTENTS

THE FIRST BOOK

ADMONITIONS USEFUL FOR A SPIRITUAL LIFE

5

THE SECOND BOOK

ADMONITIONS PERTAINING TO INWARD THINGS

THE THIRD BOOK

INTERNAL CONSOLATION

7

THE FOURTH BOOK

A DEVOUT EXHORTATION TO THE HOLY COMMUNION

The First Book

ADMONITIONS USEFUL FOR A SPIRITUAL LIFE

Chapter 1

CONTEMPT OF ALL THE VANITIES
OF THE WORLD

H E THAT FOLLOWETH ME, shall not walk in darkness" (John 8:12), saith the Lord. These are the
words of Christ, by which we are admonished how we
ought to imitate His life and manners, if we would be
enlightened and delivered from all blindness of heart.
Let therefore our chief endeavor be to meditate upon
the life of Jesus Christ.

The doctrine of Christ exceeds all the doctrine of
holy men; and he who has the Spirit will find therein
"the hidden manna" (Rev. 2:17). But many who often
hear the Gospel of Christ have little desire for it, because they "have not the Spirit of Christ" (Rom. 8:9).
But whosoever will fully and with relish understand
the words of Christ must endeavor to conform his life
wholly to the life of Christ.

What does it avail to discourse profoundly of the
Trinity if you are void of humility and are thereby displeasing to the Trinity? Surely profound words do not
make a man holy and just; but a virtuous life makes
him dear to God. I would rather feel contrition than
know the definition thereof. If you knew the whole
Bible by heart, and the sayings of all the philosophers,

11

what would all that profit you without love (I Cor. 13:2)?

"Vanity of vanities . . . all is vanity" (Eccles. 1:2), except to love God and to serve Him only. This is the highest wisdom, by the contempt of the world to press forward toward heavenly kingdoms.

Therefore it is vanity to seek after perishing riches and to trust in them. Also it is vanity to hunt after honors and to climb to high degree. It is vanity to follow the desires of the flesh, and to long after that for which you must afterward suffer grievous punishment. It is vanity to wish to live long, and to be careless to live well. It is vanity to mind only this present life, and not to foresee those things which are to come. It is vanity to set your love on that which speedily passes away, and not to hasten to where everlasting joy abides.

Call often to mind that proverb: "The eye is not satisfied with seeing, nor the ear filled with hearing" (Eccles. 1:8). Endeavor therefore to withdraw your heart from the love of visible things, and to turn yourself to things invisible. For they that follow their own sensuality defile their consciences, and lose the grace of God.

Chapter 2

HUMBLE CONCEIT OF OURSELVES

EVERY MAN naturally desires to know (Eccles. 1:13), but what does knowledge avail without the fear of God? Better, surely, is a humble laborer who serves God than a proud philosopher who, neglecting himself, studies the course of the heavens. Whoso knows himself well grows mean in his own conceit, and delights not in the praises of men. If I understood all things in the world and'had not love (I Cor. 13:2), what would that help me in the sight of God, who will judge me according to my deeds?

Cease from an inordinate desire of knowing, for therein is found much distraction and deceit. The learned are well pleased to seem so to others, and to be accounted wise. There be many things, which to know does little or nothing to profit the soul. And he is very unwise, who is intent upon any things except those which avail for his salvation. Many words do not satisfy the soul; but a good life comforts the mind, and a pure conscience gives great confidence toward God.

How much the more and the better you know, so much the more rigorously shall you therefore be judged, unless your life has been the holier. Be not therefore lifted up for any art or science, but rather fear for the knowledge that is given you.

If you think that you know many things and understand them well, know also that there are far more things which you know not. "Mind not high things" (Rom. 12:16), but rather acknowledge your own ignorance. Why will you prefer yourself before another, since there are many more learned, and more skillful in the law than you are? If you will know or learn anything profitably, desire to be unknown and to be esteemed as nothing.

The deepest and the most profitable lesson is this, the true knowledge and contempt of ourselves. It is great wisdom and high perfection to esteem nothing of ourselves, and to think always well and highly of others. If you should see another openly sin, or commit some heinous offense, you ought not to esteem yourself the better; for you know not how long you shall be able to remain in good standing. All of us are frail, but you ought not to think anyone more frail than yourself.

Chapter 3

DOCTRINE OF TRUTH

BLESSED IS THE MAN whom thou . . . teachest . . . out of thy law" (Ps. 94:12), not by figures and words that pass away, but as it is in itself. Our own opinion and our own sense often deceive us, and they discern but little.

What avails great caviling and disputing about dark and hidden things (Eccles. 3:9-11), concerning which we shall not be reproved in the Judgment because we knew them not? It is great folly to neglect the things that are profitable and necessary, and to give our minds to things curious and hurtful: "Eyes have they, but they see not" (Ps. 115:5; Mark 8:18). And what have we to do with genus and species? He to whom the eternal Word speaks is set free from many opinions. From that one Word are all things and all things speak; and this is the Beginning, which also speaks to us. No man without that understands or judges rightly. He to whom all things are one, and who draws all things to one, and sees all things in one, can be steadfast in heart, and peaceably repose in God.

O God, who art the truth, make me one with Thee in continual love! I am weary often to read and hear many things. In Thee is all that I desire and long for. Let all teachers hold their peace; let all creatures be silent in Thy sight; speak to me alone.

The more a man is at one within himself, and becomes single in heart, so much the more and higher things does he understand without labor; for he receives the light of understanding from above (Luke 10:21). A pure, sincere, and stable spirit is not distracted in a multitude of affairs, for it works all to the honor of God, and inwardly strives to be at rest from all self-seeking. Who hinders and troubles you more than the unmortified affections of your own heart? A

15

good and devout man prepares beforehand the works which he is to do before the world. Neither do they draw him according to the desires of a sinful inclination, but he himself orders them according to the decision of right reason. Who has a harder struggle than he who labors to conquer himself? This ought to be our endeavor to conquer ourselves, and daily to wax stronger than ourselves, and to make some progress for good.

All perfection in this life has some imperfection bound up with it; and no knowledge of ours is without some darkness. A humble knowledge of self is a surer way to God than a deep search after learning. Yet learning is not to be blamed, nor the mere knowledge of anything whatsoever, for knowledge is good, considered in itself, and ordained by God; but a good conscience and a virtuous life are always to be preferred before it. But because many endeavor rather to know than to live well, therefore they are often deceived, and reap either none, or scanty fruit.

Oh, if men bestowed as much labor in the rooting out of vices and planting of virtues as they do in proposing questions, there would neither be such great evils and slanders in the world, nor so much looseness among us.

Truly, when the day of judgment comes, we shall not be examined as to what we have read, but what we have done (Matt. 25); not how well we have spoken, but how we have lived.

Where are now all those masters and doctors with whom you were well acquainted while they lived and flourished in learning? Now others possess their livings, and perhaps scarcely ever think of them. In their lifetime they seemed to be somewhat, but now they are not spoken of. How quickly the glory of the world passes away (Eccles. 2:11)!

Oh, that their lives had been answerable to their learning! Then had their study and reading been to good purpose. How many perish by reason of vain learning (Titus 1:10, 11) in this world, who take little care of the serving of God! And because they rather choose to be great than humble, therefore they come to naught in their imaginations (Rom. 1:21).

He is truly great, who is great in love. He is truly great who is little in himself, and who makes no account of any height of honor (Matt. 23:11). He is truly wise who accounts all earthly things "but dung, that [he] may win Christ" (Phil. 3:8). And he is truly very learned who does the will of God and forsakes his own will.

Chapter 4

FORETHOUGHT IN ACTIONS

WE OUGHT NOT to believe every saying or suggestion but ought warily and patiently to ponder the matter with reference to God. But alas, such is our weakness, that we often believe and speak evil of others rather than good! Good men do not easily give credit to every tale; for they know that human infirmity is prone to evil (Gen. 8:21), and very subject to offend in words (James 3:2).

It is great wisdom not to be rash in actions (Prov. 19:2), nor to stand obstinately in your own conceits. It belongs also to this same wisdom not to believe everything which you hear, or to pour into the ears of others (Prov. 17:9) what you have heard or believed. Consult with a man who is wise and conscientious, and seek to be instructed by one better than yourself, rather than to follow your own inventions (Prov. 12:15).

A good life makes a man wise according to God (Prov. 15:33), and gives him experience in many things (Eccles. 1:16). The humbler a man is in himself, and the more resigned to God, the more prudent will he be in all things, and the more at peace.

Chapter 5

READ THE HOLY SCRIPTURES

TRUTH IS TO BE SOUGHT for in the Holy Scriptures, not eloquence. Holy Scripture ought to be read with the same spirit wherewith it was written (Rom. 15:4). We should rather search after profit in the Scriptures than subtilty of speech.

We ought to read devout and simple books as willingly as the high and profound. Let not the authority of the writer offend you, whether he be of great or small learning; but let the love of pure truth draw you to read (I Cor. 2:4). Search not who spoke this or that, but mark what is spoken. Men pass away, but "the truth of the Lord endureth forever" (Ps. 117:2). God speaks to us in sundry ways, without respect of persons (Rom. 2:11; 10:12).

Our own curiosity often hinders us in the reading of the Scriptures, when we desire to understand and discuss that which we should instead pass over. If you desire to reap profit, read with humility, simplicity, and faithfulness; nor ever desire the reputation of learning. Inquire willingly, and hear with silence the words of holy men. Let not the teachings of the elders displease you, for they are not recounted without cause (Eccles. 12:9).

Chapter 6

INORDINATE AFFECTIONS

WHENEVER A MAN desires anything inordinately, he is immediately disquieted within himself. The proud and covetous are never at rest. "The meek . . . shall delight themselves in the abundance of peace" (Ps. 37:11).

The man that is not yet perfectly dead to himself is quickly tempted; and he is overcome in small and trifling things. The weak in spirit, and he who is in a manner carnal and prone to things of sense can hardly withdraw himself altogether from earthly desires. Therefore he has often sadness, when he withdraws himself from them; and easily falls into indignation if anyone resists him. And if he has attained that which he lusts after, he is forthwith burdened with remorse of conscience that he followed his own passion, which helps nothing in obtaining the peace he sought for.

True peace of heart therefore is found by resisting our passions, not by obeying them. There is then no peace in the heart of a carnal man, nor in him who is given up to outward things, but in the fervent and spiritual man.

Chapter 7

VAIN HOPE AND PRIDE

VAIN IS HE who sets his hope in man (Jer. 17:5), or in creatures. Be not ashamed to serve others for the love of Jesus Christ, nor to be esteemed poor in this world.

Presume not upon yourself, but place your hope in God (Ps. 31:1). Do what lies in you, and God will assist your good will.

Trust not in your own knowledge (Jer. 9:23), nor in the subtilty of any living creature, but rather in the grace of God, who helps the humble, and humbles those that are self-presuming (I Peter 5:5).

Glory not in wealth if you have it, nor in friends because they are powerful, but in God who gives all things, and above all desires to give you Himself.

Extol not yourself for the height of your stature, or beauty of your person, which is disfigured and destroyed by a little sickness.

Take not pleasure in your natural gifts, or talent, lest thereby you displease God, whose is all the good, whatsoever you have by nature.

Esteem not yourself better than others (Exod. 3: 11), lest perhaps in the sight of God, who knows what is in man, you be accounted worse than they. Be not proud of good works (Job 9:20), for the judgments of God are different from the judgments of men, and that often offends Him which pleases men. If there be any good in you, believe better things of others, that you may preserve humility. It does not hurt to set yourself lower than all men, but it hurts exceedingly if you set yourself before even one man. Continual peace is with the humble, but in the heart of the proud is envy and frequent indignation.

Chapter 8

SHUN FAMILIARITY

LAY NOT YOUR HEART OPEN to every man (Eccles. 7:22), but discuss your affairs with the wise and him that fears God. Converse not much with young people and strangers (Prov. 5:10). Flatter not the rich, and before great personages appear not willingly. Keep company with the humble and the simple, with the devout and the virtuous, and confer with them of those things that may edify.

Desire to be familiar with God alone and His angels, and avoid the acquaintance of men. We must have love toward all, but familiarity with all is not expedient. Sometimes it turns out that a person unknown to us waxes bright from the good report of others, yet his presence darkens the eyes of the beholders. We think sometimes to please others by our company, and we begin rather to displease them with the wickedness which they discover in us.

Chapter 9

OBEDIENCE AND SUBJECTION

IT IS A VERY GREAT MATTER to stand in obedience; to live under a superior; and not to be at our own disposing. It is much safer to be in subjection than in authority.

Many are under obedience, rather for necessity than for love; such are discontented and easily murmur. Neither can they attain to freedom of mind, unless with their whole heart they put themselves under obedience for the love of God. Run hither and thither, you shall find no rest, but in humble subjection under the rule of a superior. Fancy and continual changing of places have deceived many.

True it is that everyone willingly does that which agrees with his own mind; and he is apt to affect those most that are like-minded with him. But if God is among us, we must sometimes leave even our own mind to gain the blessing of peace.

Who is so wise that he can fully know all things? Be not therefore too confident in your own mind, but be willing to hear the mind of others.

If that which you think is good, and yet you part with this very thing for God and follow another, it shall be better for you. I have often heard that it is safer to hear and to take counsel than to give it.

Each one's opinion may be good; but to refuse to yield to others when reason or a special cause requires it is a sign of pride and obstinacy.

Chapter 10

AVOID SUPERFLUITY IN WORDS

FLEE THE TUMULT of men as much as you can (Matt. 14:23); for the talk of worldly affairs is a great hindrance, although they be talked of with sincere intention; for we are quickly defiled and enthralled with vanity. Oftentimes I could wish that I had held my peace and that I had not been among men.

But why do we so willingly speak and talk with one another, when notwithstanding we seldom return to silence without hurt of conscience (Rom. 2:1)? The reason we so willingly talk is because by discoursing one with another we seek to receive comfort one of another, and desire to ease a heart overwearied with conflicting thoughts; and we very willingly talk and think of those things which we love most or desire; or of those which we feel are contrary to us. But, alas, oftentimes in vain, and to no end! For this outward comfort is the cause of no small loss of inward and divine comfort.

Therefore we must "watch and pray" (Matt. 26: 41), lest our time pass away idly. If it be lawful and expedient to speak, speak those things that may edify. An evil custom and neglect of our own good often makes us set no watch before our mouth (Ps. 141:3). Yet devout discourses of spiritual things greatly further our spiritual growth, especially when persons of one mind and spirit are gathered together in God (Acts 1:14; Rom. 15:5, 6).

Chapter 11

OBTAIN PEACE, AND PROGRESS
IN GRACE

WE MIGHT ENJOY much peace, if we would not busy ourselves with the words and deeds of other men, which pertain nothing to us. How can he abide long in peace, who thrusts himself into the cares of others, who seeks occasions abroad, who little or seldom recollects himself within his own breast?

Blessed are the singlehearted, for they shall enjoy much peace.

Why were some of the saints so perfect and contemplative? Because they studied to mortify themselves wholly to all earthly desires; and therefore they could from their very heart's core fix themselves upon God, and be free to retire within themselves.

We are too much held by our own passions, and too much troubled about transitory things. We seldom overcome even one vice perfectly, and are not set on fire to grow better every day; and therefore we remain cold and lukewarm. If we were dead unto ourselves, and not entangled within our own selves, then we should be able to relish things divine, and to know something of heavenly contemplation.

The greatest, and indeed the whole impediment is,

that we are not disentangled from our passions and lusts, neither do we endeavor to enter into the perfect path of the saints. When any small adversity meets us, we are too quickly cast down and turn to human consolation.

If we would endeavor like brave men to stand in the battle, surely we should behold above us the help of God from Heaven. For He Himself who gives us occasions to fight, to the end we may get the victory, is ready to succor those who strive and trust in His grace.

If we esteem our progress in religious life to consist only in some outward observances, our devotion will quickly have an end. But let us lay the axe to the root (Matt. 3:10), that being freed from passions we may possess our souls in peace.

If every year we would root out one vice, we should soon become perfect men. But now oftentimes we perceive it goes contrary, and that we were better and purer at the beginning of our entrance into the religious life than after many years of our profession.

Our fervor and profiting should increase daily. But now it is accounted a great matter if a man can retain but some part of his first zeal.

If we would use some little violence at the beginning, then afterward we should be able to perform all things with ease and delight. It is a hard matter to leave off that to which we are accustomed, but it is harder to go against our own wills. But if you do not overcome little and easy things, how will you overcome harder things? Resist the inclination in the very beginning and unlearn an evil habit, lest perhaps little by little it draw you into greater difficulty.

Oh, if you considered how much peace to yourself and joy to others you would procure by demeaning yourself, I believe you would be more solicitous for your spiritual progress!

Chapter 12

PROFIT OF ADVERSITY

I T IS GOOD for us that we sometimes have some wearinesses and crosses, for they often call a man back to his own heart; that he may know that he is here in banishment, and may not set his trust in any worldly thing.

It is good that we sometimes endure contradictions, and that men think ill of us; and this although we do and intend well. These things help often to humility, and defend us from vainglory. For then we the more seek God for our inward witness, when outwardly we are condemned by men and when no good is believed of us.

And therefore a man should settle himself so fully in God, that he need not seek many consolations of men.

When a man of good will is afflicted, tempted or troubled with evil thoughts, then he understands better the great need he has of God, without whom he perceives he can do nothing that is good.

Then also he sorrows, laments, and prays, by reason of the miseries he suffers. Then he is weary of living longer, and wishes that death would come, that he might be with Christ. Then also he well perceives, that perfect security and full peace cannot exist in this world.

Chapter 13

RESIST TEMPTATIONS

SO LONG AS WE LIVE in the world we cannot be without tribulation and temptation. Accordingly it is written in Job that the life of man upon earth is temptation. Everyone therefore ought to be full of care about his own temptations, and to watch in prayer lest the Devil find an advantage to deceive him. He never sleeps, but ever goes about "seeking whom he may devour" (I Peter 5:8). No man is so perfect and holy, but he sometimes has temptations; and we cannot be altogether without them.

Nevertheless temptations are often very profitable to a man, though they be troublesome and grievous; for in them a man is humbled, and purified, and instructed.

All the saints passed through many tribulations and temptations, and profited thereby. And they that could not bear temptations became reprobate, and fell away.

There is no order so holy, or place so secret, where there are not temptations or adversities. There is no man that is altogether safe from temptations while he lives on earth; for in ourselves is the root of temptation, in that we are born in the desire of evil (James 1:13, 14). When one temptation or tribulation goes away another comes. We shall always have some suffering, because we have lost the blessing of our first happiness (Gen. 3).

Many seek to flee temptations and fall more grievously into them. By flight alone we cannot overcome, but by patience and true humility we are made stronger than all our enemies.

He who only avoids them outwardly, and does not pluck them up by the roots, shall profit little. Yes, temptations will the sooner return to him, and he shall find himself in a worse case than before.

Little by little, and by patience with longsuffering (through God's help) you shall more easily overcome, than with violence and your own importunity. Often take counsel in temptation, and deal not roughly with him who is tempted; but give him comfort as you would wish for yourself.

The beginning of all evil temptations is inconstancy of mind, and small confidence in God. For as a ship without a helm is tossed to and fro with the waves, so the man who is careless, and apt to leave his purpose, is tempted in many ways (James 1:6; 3:4, 5).

Fire proves iron, and temptation a just man. We

know not oftentimes what we are able to do, but temptation shows us what we are.

Yet we must be watchful, especially in the beginning of the temptation. The enemy is then more easily overcome, if he is not permitted in any wise to enter the door of our hearts, but is resisted without the gate at his first knock. Wherefore one said: "Beginnings check, too late is physic sought." First there comes to the mind a bare thought of evil, then a strong imagination thereof, afterward delight, and an evil motion, and then consent. And so little by little our wicked enemy gets complete entrance, because he is not resisted in the beginning. And the longer a man is slow to resist, so much the weaker does he become daily in himself, and the enemy stronger against him.

Some suffer heavier temptations in the beginning of the Christian life, others in the end. Others again are much troubled almost through the whole of their lives. Some are very lightly tempted, according to the wisdom and equity of the divine appointment, which weighs the states and deserts of men, and ordains all things for the welfare of His own chosen ones.

We ought not therefore to despair when we are tempted, but the more fervently to implore God that He will vouchsafe to help us in every tribulation; who, surely, according to the word of Paul, "will with the temptation also make a way to escape, that [we] may be able to bear it" (I Cor. 10:13).

Therefore we humble ourselves "under the mighty hand of God" (I Peter 5:6) in all temptation and tribulation, for He will save and exalt the humble in spirit. In temptations and tribulations, a man is tested how much he has profited; and his reward is thereby the greater and his virtue made clearer. Neither is it a great thing if a man be devout and fervent, when he feels no affliction; but if in time of adversity he bear himself patiently, there is hope then of great progress.

Some are guarded from great temptations, and in little daily ones are often overcome; to the end that being humbled, they may never presume on themselves in great matters, who are made weak in small things.

Chapter 14

AVOID RASH JUDGMENT

TURN YOUR EYES upon your own self, and beware you judge not the deeds of other men (Matt. 7:1; Rom. 15:1). In judging others a man labors in vain, often errs, and easily sins (Eccles. 3:16), but in judging and examining himself, he always labors fruitfully.

We often judge of a thing according as we fancy it; for through private affection we easily lose true judgment. If God were always the pure intention of our desire, we should not be so easily troubled through the repugnance of our own feelings. But oftentimes something lurks within, or else meets us from without, which draws us after it.

Many secretly seek themselves in what they do, and know it not. They seem also to live in good peace of mind, when things are done according to their will and feeling. But if things happen otherwise than they desire, they are straightway moved and made sad.

From diversity of feelings and opinions dissensions oftentimes arise between friends and countrymen; between religious and devout persons (Matt. 12:25). An old habit is abandoned with difficulty (Jer. 13:23), and no man is willing to be led farther than he himself can see. If you rely more upon your own reason or industry, than upon that power which brings you under the obedience of Jesus Christ, seldom and slowly shall you be a man illuminated, because God wills us to be perfectly subject to Him, and by the fire of love to transcend all human reason.

Chapter 15

WORKS DONE FOR LOVE

FOR NO WORLDLY THING, nor for the love of any man, is any evil to be done (Matt. 18:8); but yet, for the profit of one who stands in need, a good work is sometimes without any scruple to be left undone, or rather changed for a better. For by doing this, a good work is not lost, but changed into a better. Without love the outward work profits nothing (Luke 7:47; I Cor. 13:3). But whatsoever is done of love, be it ever so little and contemptible in the sight of the world, it becomes wholly fruitful. For God weighs more the love out of which a man works, than the work which he does. He does much who loves much. He does much who does a thing well. He does well who serves the community rather than his own will (Phil. 2:17).

Oftentimes there seems to be love, and it is rather a fleshly mind; because natural inclination, self-will, hope of reward, and desire of our own interest will seldom be absent.

He who has true and perfect love seeks himself in nothing (Phil. 2:21; I Cor. 13:5), but only desires in all things the glory of God.

He also envies none; because he is in love with no private joy, neither wills he to rejoice in himself; but wishes above all good things to be made happy in the enjoyment of God (Ps. 17:15; 24:6). He attributes nothing that is good to any man, but wholly refers it to God, from whom as from the fountain all things proceed; in whom finally all the saints rest in fruition.

Oh, whoever had but one spark of true love would surely feel that all earthly things will be full of vanity!

Chapter 16

BEAR WITH THE DEFECTS OF OTHERS

THOSE THINGS that a man approves not in himself or others he ought to suffer patiently, until God orders things otherwise. Perhaps it is better so for your trial and patience, without which all our good deeds are not to be much esteemed. You ought to pray notwithstanding when you have such hindrances, that God would vouchsafe to help you, and that you may bear them contentedly (Matt. 6:13).

If one who is once or twice warned will not stay, contend not with him, but commit all to God, that His will may be done (Matt. 6:10), and He be honored in all His servants, who well know how to turn evil into good.

Endeavor to be patient in bearing with the defects and infirmities of others, of whatever sort they be; for you also have many failings which must be borne with by others (I Thess. 5:15; Gal. 6:1). If you cannot make yourself such a one as you would, how will you be able to have another in all things to your liking?

We would willingly have others perfect, and yet we correct not our own faults. We will have others severely corrected, and will not be corrected ourselves.

The large liberty of others displeases us, and yet we will not have our own desires denied us. We will have others bound down by ordinances, and we ourselves endure no further restraint.

And thus it appears, how seldom we weigh our neighbor in the same balance with ourselves.

If all men were perfect, what should we then have to suffer of others for God? But now God has thus ordered it, that we may learn to bear one another's burdens (Gal. 6:2). No man is without fault, no man without his burden, no man sufficient of himself, no man wise enough of himself. But we ought to bear with one another, comfort one another, help, instruct, and admonish one another (I Cor. 12:25; I Thess. 5:14).

Occasions of adversity discover best how great virtue each one has. For such occasions do not make a man frail, but they reveal what sort he is.

Chapter 17

A RETIRED LIFE

YOU MUST LEARN to break down your own self in many things, if you will have peace and concord with others (Gal. 6:1). It is no small matter to dwell in religious communities or in a congregation, to converse therein without complaint, and to persevere therein faithfully unto death (Luke 16:10). Blessed is he who has lived well there, and ended happily.

If you will stand fast as you ought, and grow in grace, esteem yourself as an exile and a stranger upon earth (I Peter 2:11). You must be made a fool for Christ's sake (I Cor. 4:10), if you desire to lead a Christian life.

He who seeks anything else but merely God, and the welfare of his own soul, shall find nothing but tribulation and sorrow (Eccles. 1:17, 18). Neither can he stand long in peace who labors not to be the least, and subject unto all.

You came to serve, not to rule (Matt. 20:26). Know that you were called to suffer and to labor, not to be idle, and spend your time in talk. Here therefore men are proved as gold in the furnace. Here no man can stand, unless he be willing to humble himself with his whole heart for the love of God.

Chapter 18

EXAMPLES OF THE FATHERS

LOOK UPON the examples of the holy Fathers, in whom true perfection and religion shined (Heb. 11); and you shall see how little, almost nothing, which we do in these days. Alas, what is our life in comparison!

The saints and friends of Christ served Him in hunger and thirst, in cold and nakedness, in labor and weariness, in watchings and fastings, in prayers and holy meditations, in many persecutions and reproaches (II Cor. 11:26, 27).

Oh, how many and grievous tribulations did the apostles, martyrs, and all the rest suffer, who willed to follow the steps of Christ! For they hated their lives in this world, that they might keep them unto life eternal (John 12:25).

How strict and self-renouncing a life did those Fathers lead in the wilderness (Matt: 7:14)! How long and grievous temptations they suffered! How often they were assaulted by the enemy! What frequent and fervent prayers they offered to God! How great zeal and ardor they had for their spiritual progress! How fierce a war they waged for the taming of their faults! How pure and upright an intention they kept toward God!

Through the day they labored, and in the night they attended to prayer, although when they labored they ceased not from mental prayer.

All their time they spent with profit; every hour seemed short for the service of God; and by reason of the great sweetness they felt in contemplation, they even forgot the need of bodily refreshment.

All riches, dignities, honors, friends, and kinsfolk they renounced (Matt. 19:29). They desired to have nothing which pertained to the world; they scarcely took things necessary for the sustenance of life; they grieved to serve their bodies even in necessity. Therefore they were poor in earthly things, but rich exceedingly in grace and virtues (II Cor. 6:10). Outwardly they were destitute, but inwardly they were refreshed with grace and divine consolation.

To the world they were strangers, but near and familiar friends to God (James 4:4). They seemed to themselves as nothing, and to this present world despicable; but they were precious and beloved in the eyes of God. They stood firm in true humility, lived in simple obedience, walked in love and patience; and therefore they profited daily in the Spirit, and obtained great favor with God.

They were given for an example to all men. And they should more provoke us to profit well, than the number of the lukewarm to make us remiss.

Oh, how great was the fervor of the apostles in the beginning of their holy institution! How great was the devotion of their prayer! How great their ambition to excel others in virtue! What mighty discipline was then in force! How great reverence and obedience flourished in all things.

Their footsteps yet remaining do testify that they were indeed holy men who, fighting so valiantly, trod the world under their feet.

Now, he is accounted great who is not a transgressor, and who can with patience endure that which he has undertaken. Oh, the lukewarmness and negligence of our own condition, that we so quickly decline from the ancient fervor, and are come to be weary of life through sloth and lukewarmness!

Would to God the desire to grow in virtues did not wholly sleep in us, who have often seen the many examples of the devout!

Chapter 19

EXERCISES OF A RELIGIOUS PERSON

THE LIFE of a good religious person ought to be mighty in all virtues (Matt. 5:48), that he may inwardly be such as outwardly he seems to men. And with reason there ought to be much more within than is perceived without. For God beholds us (Ps. 33:13; Heb. 4:13), whom we are bound most highly to reverence, wherever we are, and to walk in purity (Ps. 15:2) like angels in His sight.

We ought daily to renew our purpose and to stir up ourselves to fervor, as though we had for the first time today entered the Christian life, and to say: "Help me, O Lord God, in this my good purpose, and in Thy holy service; and grant that I may now this day begin perfectly, for that which I have done hitherto is as nothing."

According to our purpose shall be the course of our spiritual profiting; and much diligence is necessary to him who will profit much.

And if he who firmly purposes often fails, what shall he do who seldom, or with little firmness, purposes anything? It turns out in various ways that we leave off our purpose; yet the light omission of spiritual exercises seldom passes without some loss to our souls. The purpose of just men depends not upon their own wisdom, but upon God's grace; on whom too they always rely for whatever they take in hand. For man proposes but God disposes (Prov. 16:9); neither is the way of man in himself.

If an accustomed exercise be sometimes omitted, either for some act of piety, or profit to my brother, it may easily afterward be recovered. But if out of a slothful mind, or out of carelessness, we lightly forsake the same, it is blameworthy enough, and will be felt to be hurtful.

Let us do the best we can, we shall still easily fail in many things (Eccles. 7:20). Yet we must always purpose some certain course, and especially against those failings which most of all hinder us.

We must diligently search into and set in order both the outward and the inner man, because both of them are of importance to our progress in godliness.

If you cannot continually recollect yourself, yet do it sometimes, at least once a day, namely, in the morning or at evening. In the morning fix your good purpose; and at evening examine your ways, how you have behaved yourself this day in word, deed, and thought (Deut. 4); for in these perhaps you have oftentimes offended both God and your neighbor.

"Gird up now thy loins like a man" (Job 38:3) against the vile assaults of the Devil; bridle your gluttony and you shall the better bridle all the desire of the flesh. Never be entirely idle; but either be reading, or writing, or praying, or meditating, or endeavoring something for the public good. Bodily exercises, nevertheless, must be used with discretion; neither are they to be practiced of all men alike.

Those exercises which are not common are not to be exposed to public view; for things private are practiced more safely at home. Nevertheless you must beware that you are not slack in those which are common, and more ready for those which concern yourself only. But having fully and faithfully accomplished all which you are bound and enjoined to do, if you have any spare time, do as your devotion shall desire.

All cannot use one kind of spiritual exercise, but one is more useful for this person, another for that. In the time of temptation we have need of some, and of others in time of peace and quietness. Some we like to have in mind when we are sad, and others when we rejoice in the Lord.

Chapter 20

LOVE OF SOLITUDE AND SILENCE

SEEK A CONVENIENT TIME (Eccles. 3:1) to yourself and meditate often upon God's lovingkindnesses. Forsake curious questionings, but read diligently matters which rather yield contrition to your heart than occupation to your head.

If you will withdraw yourself from speaking vainly and from gadding idly, as also from hearkening after new things and rumors, you shall find time enough and suitable for meditation on good things.

The greatest saints avoided, when they could, the society of men (Heb. 11:38), and did rather choose to live to God in secret.

A certain one has said: "As oft as I have been among men, I returned home less a man that I was before." And this we often find true, when we talk long together. It is easier altogether to hold one's peace, than not speak more words than we ought. It is easier for a man to keep himself well at home than when he is abroad.

He therefore who intends to attain to the more inward and spiritual things of religion must with Jesus depart from the multitude (Matt. 5:1).

No man safely appears abroad, but he who gladly hides himself. No man safely speaks, but he who willingly holds his peace (Eccles. 3:7). No man safely rules, but he who is willingly in subjection. No man safely commands, but he who has learned well to obey. No man safely rejoices, unless he has within him the witness of a good conscience (Acts 23:1).

And yet always the security of the saints was full of the fear of God. Neither were they the less anxious and humble in themselves, for they shined outwardly with great virtues and grace. But the security of bad men arises from pride and presumption, and in the end it turns to a man's own deceiving.

Never promise yourself security in this life, although you seem to be a good religious man, or a devout hermit. Oftentimes those who have been greater in the esteem of men have fallen into the heavier peril by overmuch self-confidence. Wherefore to many it is more profitable not to be altogether free from temptations, but to be often assaulted, lest they should be too secure, and so perhaps be puffed up with pride, or else too freely yield to worldly comforts.

Oh, how good a conscience would he keep, who did never seek after transitory joy, nor ever entangle himself with this world! Oh, how great peace and quietness would he possess, who did cut off all vain anxiety, and think only upon divine things, and such as are profitable for his soul, and place all his hope in God!

No man is worthy of heavenly comfort, unless he has diligently exercised himself in holy contrition. If you desire to be truly contrite in heart, enter into your secret chamber and shut out the tumults of the world.

In your chamber you shall find what you shall too often lose abroad (Matt. 6:6). Your chamber, if you continue therein, grows sweet; and if you keep it little, it begets weariness. If in the beginning of your religious life you are content to remain in it, and keep to it well, it will afterward be a dear friend and a very pleasant comfort. In silence and in stillness a devout soul profits and learns the hidden things of the Scriptures. There he finds rivers of tears, wherein he may every night (Ps. 6:6) wash and cleanse himself, that he may be more familiar with his Creator, the farther off he lives from all worldly disquiet. Whoso therefore withdraws himself from his acquaintances and friends, God will draw near unto him with His holy angels.

Why are you desirous to see that which you may not have? "The world passeth away, and the lust thereof" (I John 2:17). Our sensual desires draw us to rove abroad; but when the hour is past, what do you carry home but heaviness of conscience and distraction of heart? A merry going forth brings often a sad returning, and a merry evening makes a sad morning (Prov. 14:13). So all carnal joy enters gently, but in the end bites and stings to death (Prov. 23:7, 31, 32).

What can you see elsewhere, which you see not here (Eccles. 1:10)? Behold the Heaven and the earth and all the elements, for of these are all things created.

What can you see anywhere that can long continue under the sun? You think perchance to satisfy yourself, but you never attain it. Should you see all things present before your eyes, what were it but an empty vision (Eccles. 3:11)?

Lift up your eyes (Ps. 121:1) to God in the highest, and pray Him to pardon your sins and negligences. Leave vain things to the vain; but be intent upon those things which God has commanded you. Shut your door and call unto Jesus, your Beloved. Stay with Him in your closet; for you shall not find elsewhere so great peace. If you had not gone abroad and hearkened to idle rumors, you would have remained in happy peace. But since you delight sometimes to hear new things, it is but fit you suffer disquietude of heart therefrom.

Chapter 21

CONTRITION OF HEART

IF YOU WILL MAKE any progress keep yourself in the fear of God (Prov. 19:23), and affect not too much liberty, but restrain all your senses under discipline, and give not yourself over to foolish mirth. Give yourself to contrition of heart, and you shall find devotion. Contrition lays open many good things, which distraction is wont quickly to destroy.

It is a wonder that any man can ever perfectly rejoice in this life, who considers and weighs his own state of exile and the many perils of his soul. Through levity of heart, and small concern for our failings, we become insensible of the sorrows of our souls; but oftentimes we vainly laugh, when we justly ought to weep. There is no true liberty or right joy but in the fear of God accompanied with a good conscience.

Happy is he who can cast off all distracting hindrances, and gather himself to the one single purpose of holy contrition. Happy is he who can put away from him all that may defile his conscience or burden it.

Strive manfully; one habit is vanquished of another.

If you can let others alone in their works, they likewise shall gladly let you alone in yours. Busy not yourself in matters of others; neither entangle yourself with the affairs of your superiors. Have an eye to yourself first, and especially admonish your own self before all your beloved friends.

If you have not the favor of men, be not grieved at it (Gal. 1:10); but take this to heart, that you keep yourself so warily and circumspectly as it becomes the servant of God and a devout man to behave. It is better oftentimes and safer that a man should not have many consolations in this life (Ps. 76:5), especially such as are according to the flesh. But that we have no divine consolations at all, or very seldom feel them, the fault is ours; because we seek not after contrition of heart, nor do altogether forsake vain and outward comforts.

Know that you are unworthy of divine consolation, and that you are rather worthy of much tribulation. When a man is perfectly contrite, then is the whole world grievous and bitter unto him (Judg. 2:4; 20:26; II Sam. 12:17).

A good man finds always sufficient cause for mourning and weeping. For whether he considers himself or thinks of his neighbor, he knows that none lives here without tribulation. And the more thoroughly a man considers himself, so much the more he sorrows.

Matter of just sorrow and inward contrition are our faults and sins, in which we lie so enwrapped that rarely have we power to contemplate the things of Heaven.

If you oftener think of death (Eccles. 7:1, 2) than of living long, there is no question but you would be

46

more zealous to amend. If also you considered the penalties that are to be in Hell (Matt. 25:41), I believe you would willingly undergo labor and sorrow, and not be afraid of the greatest austerity. But because these things do not enter your heart, and you still love those things which flatter, therefore you remain cold and very sluggish.

It is often our want of spirit which makes our miserable body so easily complain. Pray therefore unto the Lord with all humility, that He will give you the spirit of contrition. And say with the psalmist: "Thou feedest them with the bread of tears; and givest them tears to drink in great measure" (Ps. 80:5).

Chapter 22

HUMAN MISERY

MISERABLE YOU ARE, wherever you be, or whither you turn, unless you turn to God.

Why are you troubled when things succeed not as you desire? Who is he who has all things according to his mind (Eccles. 6:2)? Neither I nor you, nor any man upon earth. There is none in this world, even though he be king or pope, without some tribulation or perplexity. Who is he who has the better lot? Assuredly he who is able to suffer something for God.

Many weak and unstable persons say, Behold, what

a happy life that man leads (Luke 12:19), how wealthy, how great he is, how powerful and exalted! But look to the riches of Heaven, and you shall see that these temporal things are nothing, but are very uncertain, and rather burdensome than otherwise, because they are never possessed without anxiety and fear. Man's happiness consists not in having abundance of temporal goods (Prov. 19:1), but a moderate portion is sufficient for him.

Truly it is misery to live upon the earth (Job 19:1; Eccles. 2:17). The more spiritual a man desires to be, the more bitter does this present life become to him, because he perceives better and sees more clearly the defects of human corruption. For to eat and to drink, to sleep and to wake, to labor and to rest, and to be subject to the other necessities of nature, is truly a great misery and affliction to a devout man, who would gladly be set loose, and free from all sin. For the inner man is much weighed down with bodily necessities in this world. Therefore the psalmist prays with great devotion to be enabled to be free from them, saying: "O bring thou me out of my distresses" (Ps. 25:17).

But woe unto them who know not their own misery; and a greater woe unto them who love this miserable and corruptible life (Rom. 8:22)! For some there be who so much dote upon it, that although by labor they can scarcely get mere necessities, yet if they might be able to live here always, they would care nothing at all for the kingdom of God. O senseless and unbelieving in heart, who lie so deeply sunk in earth, that they can relish nothing but carnal things (Rom. 8:5)! But,

48

miserable men, they shall in the end realize how vile and worthless that was with which they were in love.

The saints of God and all the devout friends of Christ regarded not those things which pleased the flesh, nor those which flourished in this present time, but all their hope and endeavor panted after the good things which are eternal (I Peter 1:4; Heb. 11:26). Their whole desire was carried upward to things durable and invisible, that the desire of things visible might not draw them to things below.

My brother, lose not your confidence of making progress toward the things of the Spirit; you still have time, the hour is not yet past (Rom. 13:11; Heb. 10:35). Why will you defer your good purpose from day to day? Arise and in this very instant begin, and say, Now is the time to be doing, now is the time to be fighting, now is the time to be amending myself.

When you are ill at ease and much troubled, then is the time to gain most blessing. You must pass through fire and water before you come to the place of refreshing. Unless you do violence to yourself, you shall never get the victory over wickedness.

So long as we carry about us this frail body, we can never be without sin, or live without weariness and pain. We would gladly have rest from all misery, but seeing by sin we have lost our innocency, we have lost also the true happiness (Rom. 7:24; Gen. 3:17). Therefore, it becomes us to keep hold on patience, and to wait for the mercy of God "until these calamities be overpast" (Ps. 57:1) and "mortality be swallowed up of life" (II Cor. 5:4).

Oh, how great is human frailty, which is always prone to evil (Gen. 6:5)! Today you confess your sins, and tomorrow you commit the very same sins you have confessed today. Now you purpose to take heed, and after an hour you behave yourself as though you had never had any such purpose at all. Therefore we have good cause to humble ourselves and never to have any great conceit of ourselves, since we are so frail and so inconstant. Besides, that may quickly be lost by our own negligence, which, by the grace of God, with much labor we have scarcely at length obtained.

What will become of us in the end, who so early wax lukewarm? Woe be unto us, if we will thus give ourselves unto ease, as if already there were peace and safety, when as yet there appears no trace of true holiness in our conversation!

It would be very profitable for us like young beginners to be newly instructed again to good life (Heb. 5:12), if haply there might be some hope of future amendment and greater spiritual profiting.

Chapter 23

MEDITATION ON DEATH

VERY QUICKLY there will be an end of you here (Job 9:25, 26; 14:1, 2; Luke 12:20; Heb. 9:27); look what will become of you in another world. Today man is; and tomorrow he appears not. And when he is taken away from sight, he also quickly passes out of mind.

Oh, dullness and hardness of man's heart, which thinks only upon the present, and does not rather care for what is to come! You ought so to order yourself in every act and thought, as if today you were on the point to die. If you had a good conscience you would not greatly fear death (Luke 12:37). It were better to avoid sins than to flee death. If today you are not prepared, how can you be tomorrow? Tomorrow is uncertain, and how do you know if you shall have a tomorrow?

What avails it to live long, when we amend ourselves so little! Alas, length of days does not always amend us, but often rather increases our fault! Oh, that we had well spent but one day in this world! Many there are who count the years of their life in religion; and yet slender oftentimes is the fruit of amendment.

Blessed is he who always has the hour of his death before his eyes (Eccles. 7:1), and daily prepares himself to die. If at any time you have seen another man die, remember you must also pass the same way (Heb. 9:27). When it is morning, think you might not come to eventide. And when it is evening, dare not to promise yourself the morning. Always, therefore, be ready, and so live that death may never take you unprepared, for many die suddenly. When that last hour shall come, you will have a far different opinion of your whole past life and regret you have been so careless and remiss.

How wise and happy is he who now labors to be in life as he wishes to be found at his death! A perfect contempt of the world, a fervent desire to go forward in virtue, the love of discipline, the painfulness of repentance, the readiness of obedience, the denying of ourselves, and the bearing of any adversity whatever for the love of Christ, will give us great confidence that we shall die happily.

You can do many good things while in health, but when you are sick, I see not what you are able to do. Few grow better by sickness; as also they who wander much on pilgrimage, seldom thereby become holy.

Put not your confidence in friends and kindred, neither put off your welfare till hereafter; for men will forget you sooner than you are aware of. It is better to look to it and do some good beforehand than to hope in other men's help (Isa. 30:5; 31:1; Jer. 17:5; 48:7; Matt. 6:20).

Time is very precious. "Behold, now is the accepted time; behold, now is the day of salvation" (II Cor. 6:2). But, alas, that you should not spend this time to more profit, wherein you might learn that by which you shall live eternally hereafter! The time will come, when you shall desire one day or hour to amend in, and I know not that you will obtain it. Ah, beloved, from how great danger will you be able to free yourself, from how great fear deliver yourself, if only you will be ever fearful and mindful of death!

Labor now to live so that in the hour of death you

may rather rejoice than fear. Learn now to die to the world, that you may then begin to live with Christ (Rom. 6:8). Learn now to forsake all things (Luke 14:33) that you may then freely go to Christ. Chastise your body now by repentance (I Cor. 9:27) that you may then have sure confidence.

Ah, fool, why do you think to live long, when you have not one day that is safe? How many have been deceived and suddenly snatched from the body! How often have you heard them saying, That man has fallen by the sword; that man has drowned; that man by falling from a height has broken his neck; that man died while eating; that man has come to his end while playing! One perished by fire, another by the steel, another of the plague, another at the hands of robbers; and thus death comes to all, and man's life suddenly passes away like a shadow (Job 14:2). Who shall remember you when you are dead?

Do now, my beloved, whatever you are able to do; for you know not when you shall die, neither what shall befall you after your death. While you have time, heap unto yourself everlasting riches (Matt. 6:20; Gal. 6:8). Think on nothing but your salvation; care for nothing but the things of God. Keep yourself as a stranger and pilgrim upon the earth (I Peter 2:11), and as one to whom the affairs of this world do not belong. Keep your heart free, and lifted up to God, because you have here "no continuing city" (Heb. 13:14).

Chapter 24

JUDGMENT, AND THE PUNISHMENT OF SINNERS

IN ALL THINGS look to the end; and how you will stand before that just Judge (Heb. 10:31) from whom nothing is hidden, who is not appeased with gifts, nor admits excuses, but will judge according to right.

Oh, wretched and foolish sinner, who sometimes are in terror at the countenance of an angry man, what answer will you make to God who knows all your wickedness (Job 9:2)? Why do you not provide for yourself against the day of judgment, when no man can be excused or defended by another, but everyone shall be a sufficient burden for himself? Now is your toil fruitful, your weeping acceptable (II Cor. 6:4), your groaning audible, your grief commends you to God, and purges your soul.

The patient man has a great and wholesome purification (James 1:4). Though he receives injuries, yet he grieves more for the malice of the other than for his own wrong. He prays willingly for his adversaries (Luke 23:34; Acts 7:60), and from his heart forgives their offenses. He is not slow to ask forgiveness from others; is more quickly moved to compassion than to anger; often does violence to himself, and labors to bring the flesh wholly into subjection to the spirit.

It is better to purge out our sins, and cut off our

vices here, than to keep them to be purged away hereafter. Verily, we deceive our own selves through the inordinate love we have for the flesh.

In what things a man has sinned, in the same shall he be grievously punished. There shall the slothful be pricked forward with burning goads, and the gluttons be tormented with vast thirsts and hunger. There shall the luxurious and lovers of pleasures be bathed in burning pitch and stinking brimstone; and the envious, like raging dogs, shall howl for very grief. There is no sin but shall have its proper torment. There the proud shall be filled with all confusion; the covetous shall be pinched with miserable penury.

There one hour of pain shall be severer than a hundred years of the severest discipline here! There is no quiet, no comfort for the damned; yet here we have some respite of our labors and enjoy the comfort of our friends.

Be anxious and sorrowful because of your sins now, that at the day of judgment you may be secure with the blessed.

For then shall the righteous with great boldness stand against such as have straitened and oppressed them. Then shall he stand for judgment, who now humbly submits himself to the judgments of men. Then shall the poor and humble have great confidence, but the proud man shall be compassed with fear on every side. Then will it be seen that he was wise in this world, who had learned for Christ to be a fool and despised (I Cor. 4:10).

Then shall every affliction patiently suffered delight

us, when "all iniquity shall stop her mouth" (Ps. 107:42). Then shall every devout man be glad, and every profane one shall mourn. Then the flesh which has been beaten down shall rejoice more than if it had been always nourished in delicacies (II Cor. 4:17). Then shall the poor attire shine gloriously, and the finely wrought raiment shall grow dim. Then the poor cottage shall be more commended than the gilded palace. Then will constant patience avail us more than all the power of the world.

Then simple obedience shall be more highly extolled than all worldly craftiness (Isa. 29:19). Then shall a good and clear conscience rejoice a man more than learned philosophy. Then shall the contempt of riches weigh more than all the worlding's treasure. Then will you be more comforted that you have prayed devoutly than that you have fared daintily. Then will you be more glad you have kept silence than that you have talked much. Then will good works avail more than many fair words. Then a strict life and severe discipline will be more pleasing than all earthly delight.

"All is vanity" (Eccles. 1:2), but to love God and to serve Him only. For he who loves God with all his heart is neither afraid of death, nor punishment, nor of judgment, nor of Hell; for perfect love gives secure access to God (Rom. 8:39). But he who delights still to sin, what marvel is it if he fears both death and judgment? Yet it is good, although love be not forceful enough to call you back from sin, that at least the fear of Hell should restrain you. Nay, he who lays aside the fear of God can never continue long in good standing, but runs quickly into the snares of the Devil.

Chapter 25

ZEALOUS AMENDMENTS OF LIFE

B E WATCHFUL AND DILIGENT in the service of God (II Tim. 4:5). Be fervent to go forward (Matt. 5:48), for shortly you shall receive the reward of your labors; there shall not then be any fear or sorrow in your coasts. Labor now but a little and you shall find great rest, yea, perpetual joy (Rev. 21:4; 22:3). If you continue faithful and fervent in doing good, no doubt God will be faithful and liberal in rewarding you (Matt. 25:23). You ought to have a good hope (Rom. 5:5) that you will come to the palm of victory, but you must not be secure lest you wax either slothful or proud.

When one who was in anxiety of mind, often wavering between fear and hope, did once, being overcome with grief, prostrate himself in a church before a certain altar in prayer, and pondered thus within himself, saying, "Oh, if I knew that I should yet persevere!" he presently heard within him a divine answer, "If you did know this, what would you do? Do now what you would do then, and you shall be perfectly secure." And being therewith comforted and strengthened, he committed himself wholly to the divine will, and that anxious tossing ceased. And he willed not to search curiously, to know what things should befall him, but rather labored to seek out what was the acceptable and perfect will of God (Rom. 12:2) for the beginning and the accomplishing of every good work.

"Trust in the Lord, and do good; so shalt thou dwell in the land, and verily thou shalt be fed" (Ps. 37:3).

There is one thing that draws many back from spiritual progress and fervent improvement; dread of the difficulty, or rather the labor of the combat. However, they improve most in virtues, who strive like men to overcome those things which are most grievous and contrary to them. For a man improves more and wins fuller grace, where he more overcomes himself and mortifies himself in spirit. Howbeit all men have not equally much to overcome and put to death. Yet he who is diligent and zealous, though he have more passions, shall be mightier to go forward, than another who is of a more obedient temper but less fervent in the pursuit of virtues.

Two things especially help to great improvement— to withdraw ourselves from that to which nature is viciously inclined; and to labor earnestly for that good whereof a man is the more in need.

Be careful also the more to shun and conquer those things in yourself, which commonly displease you in others.

Gather some profit wherever you are, so that if you see or hear any good examples, kindle yourself to the imitation thereof. But if you observe anything worthy of reproof, beware you do not the same. And if at any time you have done it, labor quickly to improve yourself. As your eye observes others (Matt. 7:3), so are you observed by others.

How sweet and pleasant a thing it is to see brethren fervent and devout, obedient and well disciplined (Eph. 5; Ps. 133)! How sad and grievous it is to see them walk disorderly, not applying themselves to that for which they are called! How hurtful when they neglect the purpose of their calling and busy themselves in things not committed to their care!

Be mindful of the purpose you have embraced, and set always before you the vision of the Crucified. You have good cause to be ashamed in looking upon the life of Jesus Christ, seeing you have not as yet endeavored to conform yourself more unto Him, though you have been a long time in the way of God. A religious person who exercises himself seriously and devoutly in the most holy life and passion of our Lord shall there abundantly find whatever is profitable and necessary for him, neither shall he need to seek any better thing, besides Jesus. Oh, if Jesus crucified would come into our hearts (Gal. 2:16; 6:14), how quickly and fully should we be taught!

A truly Christian person takes and bears well all that is commanded him. A careless and lukewarm Christian has tribulation upon tribulation, and on all sides suffers affliction, for he is void of inward consolation, and that which is outward he is forbidden to seek. A Christian who lives not according to discipline lies open to grievous ruin. He who seeks what is easier and more lax shall always be in difficulties; for one thing or other will displease him.

Oh, that nothing else lay upon us to do, but with our mouth and whole heart to praise our Lord God! Oh, that you might never have need to eat, nor drink, nor sleep, but might always praise God, and only employ yourself in spiritual exercises! Then you would be much happier than now, when for some necessity or other you are in bondage to the flesh. Would God these necessities were only the spiritual banquets of the soul, which, alas, we taste seldom enough!

When a man comes to that state, that he seeks not his comfort from any creature, then God first begins to be altogether sweet to him. Then shall he be contented with whatever befalls him in this world. Then shall he neither rejoice in great matters, nor be sorrowful for small, but entirely and confidently he commits himself to God, who is unto him all in all (Rom. 11:36; I Cor. 8:6; 12:6; 15:28); to whom assuredly nothing perishes or dies, but all things do live unto Him, and serve Him without delay.

Remember always your end, and how that time lost returns not. Without care and diligence you shall never get virtue. If you begin to wax lukewarm (Rev. 3:16), it will be evil with you. But if you give yourself to fervor, you shall find much peace, and feel lighter toil through the assistance of God's grace and the love of virtue. A man fervent and diligent is prepared for all things.

It is harder toil to resist vices and passions than to sweat in bodily labors. He who avoids not small faults, little by little falls into greater. You will always rejoice in the evening if you spend the day profitably.

The Second Book

ADMONITIONS PERTAINING TO INWARD THINGS

Chapter 1

THE INWARD LIFE

THE KINGDOM OF GOD is within you" (Luke 17:21), saith the Lord. Turn with your whole heart (Joel 2:12) unto the Lord, and forsake this wretched world, and your soul shall find rest. Learn to despise outward things, and to give yourself to things inward, and you shall perceive the kingdom of God to come in you. "For the kingdom of God is . . . peace, and joy in the Holy Ghost" (Rom. 14:17), which is not given to the unholy. Christ will come to you and show you His consolation, if you prepare for Him a worthy abode within. All His glory and beauty are from within (Ps. 45:13), and there He delights Himself. He often visits the inward man, and has sweet discourse, pleasant solace, much peace, familiarity exceedingly wonderful with him.

O faithful soul, make ready your heart for this Bridegroom, that He may vouchsafe to come and dwell within you! For thus saith He: "If a man love me, he will keep my words . . . and we will come unto him, and make our abode with him" (John 14:23).

Give therefore a place unto Christ, and deny entrance to all others. When you have Christ, you are rich, and have enough. He Himself will be your provider and faithful steward in all things, so that you need not trust in men. For men soon change, and quickly fail; but "Christ abideth forever" (John 12:34) and stands by us firmly unto the end. There is no great trust to be put in a frail and mortal man (Jer. 17:5), even though he be profitable and dear unto us. Neither ought we to be much grieved if sometimes he cross and contradict us. They that today are with you, tomorrow may be against you; and often again they turn around like the wind.

Put all your trust in God (I Peter 5:7), let Him be your fear and your love. He Himself shall answer for you, and will do in all things what is best for you. You have not a continuing city here (Heb. 13:14), and wherever you are, you are a foreigner and pilgrim (Heb. 11:13). Neither shall you ever have rest unless you be most inwardly united unto Christ. Why do you here look about, since this is not the place of your rest? Heaven ought to be your dwelling place (Phil. 3:20), and all earthly things are to be looked upon as it were by the way. All things are passing away, and you together with them. Beware you do not cleave unto them, lest you be caught and perish. Let your meditation be on the Most High, and your prayer for mercy directed unto Christ without ceasing.

If you cannot contemplate high and heavenly things, rest yourself in the passion of Christ, and dwell willingly in His sacred wounds. For if you flee devoutly unto the wounds and precious marks of the Lord Jesus, you shall feel great strengthening in tribulation. Neither will you care for the slights of men, and will easily bear words of detraction. Christ was also in the world, despised of men, and in greatest necessity, forsaken by His acquaintances and friends, in the midst of slanderers. Christ willed to suffer and be despised (Matt. 12:24; 16:21; John 15:20); and do you dare complain of any man? Christ had adversaries and backbiters; and do you wish to have all men your friends and benefactors? Whence shall your patience attain her crown (II Tim. 2:5) if no adversity befall you? If you are willing to suffer nought that is against you, how will you be the friend of Christ? Be strong with Christ, and for Christ, if you desire to reign with Christ. If you had but once perfectly entered into the secrets of the Lord Jesus, and tasted a little of His ardent love, then you would care nothing for your own convenience, or inconvenience, but rather would rejoice at slander, for the love of Jesus makes a man despise himself.

A lover of Jesus and of the truth, and a true inward Christian, and one free from unruly affections, can freely turn himself unto God, and lift himself above himself in spirit, and with profit remain at rest.

He to whom all things taste as they are, and not as they are said or esteemed to be, is truly wise, and taught rather of God than men (Isa. 54:13). He who can live inwardly, and make small reckoning of things without, neither seeks places, nor waits for times, for performing of religious exercises. A spiritual man quickly recollects himself, because he never pours out himself wholly to outward things. He is not hindered by outward labor, or business which may be necessary for the time, but as things fall out, so he accommodates himself to them. He who is well ordered and disposed within himself cares not for the strange and perverse behavior of men. A man is hindered and distracted in proportion as he draws outward things to himself.

If it were well with you, and you were well purified from sin, all things would fall out to you for good (Rom. 8:28), and to your advancement in holiness. For this cause many things displease and often trouble you, because you are not yet perfectly dead unto yourself, nor separated from all earthly things. Nothing so defiles and entangles the heart of man as the impure love of creatures. If you refuse to be comforted from without, you will be able to contemplate the things of Heaven, and often to rejoice within.

Chapter 2

HUMBLE SUBMISSION

COUNT NOT of great importance who is for you, or against you (Rom. 8:31; I Cor. 4:3), but let this be your aim and care, that God be with you in every thing you do. Have a good conscience, and God shall defend you (Ps. 28:7). For whom God wills to help, no man's perverseness shall be able to hurt. If you know how to be silent and suffer, without doubt you shall see the help of the Lord. He Himself knows the time and manner of delivering you, and therefore you ought to resign yourself unto Him. It belongs to God to help, and to deliver from all confusion.

It is often very profitable to keep us humble, that others know and rebuke our faults. When a man humbles himself for his faults, then he easily pacifies others, and lightly satisfies those who are offended with him.

God protects the humble and delivers him (James 4:6; Job 5:11). He loves and comforts the humble; unto the humble man He inclines Himself; unto the humble He gives great grace; and after his humiliation He raises him to glory. Unto the humble He reveals His secrets (Matt. 11:25), and sweetly draws and invites him unto Himself. The humble man, though he suffer confusion, is yet perfectly in peace; for he rests on God and not on the world.

Do not think that you have made any progress, unless you esteem yourself inferior to all.

Chapter 3

A GOOD, PEACEABLE MAN

KEEP YOURSELF FIRST in peace, and then you shall be able to pacify others. A peaceable man does more good than he who is well learned. A passionate man turns even good into evil, and easily believes evil.

A good, peaceable man turns all things to good. He who is well in peace is not suspicious of any (I Cor. 13:5). But he who is discontented and troubled is tossed with divers suspicions. He is neither quiet himself, nor suffers others to be quiet. He often speaks that which he ought not to speak; and omits that which it were more expedient for him to speak. He considers what others are bound to do (Matt. 7:3), and neglects that which he is bound to do himself.

First, therefore, be zealous over yourself (Acts 1:7; 22:3; John 21:22), and then you may justly be zealous toward your neighbor. You know how to excuse and color your own deeds, but you are not willing to receive the excuses of others. It were more just that you should accuse yourself, and excuse your brother. If you will be borne withal, bear also with another (Gal. 6:2; I Cor. 13:7).

Behold, how far off you are from true love and humility, which know not how to be angry with any, or to be moved with indignation, but only against its own self! It is no great matter to associate with the good and gentle, for this is naturally pleasing to all, and everyone willingly enjoys peace, and loves those best who agree with him. But to be able to live peaceably with hard, and perverse, or undisciplined persons, is a great grace, and an exceedingly commendable and manly deed.

Some there are who keep themselves in peace, and are in peace also with others. And there are some who neither are in peace themselves, nor leave others in peace. They are troublesome to others, but always more troublesome to themselves. And there are some who keep themselves in peace, and study to bring others unto peace.

Nevertheless, our whole peace in this miserable life consists rather in humble sufferance than in not feeling adversities. Whosoever knows best how to suffer will keep the greatest peace. That man is conqueror of himself, and lord of the world, the friend of Christ, and heir of Heaven.

Chapter 4

SIMPLICITY AND PURITY

BY TWO WINGS a man is lifted up from things earthly; namely, by simplicity and purity. Simplicity ought to be in our intention; purity in our affection. Simplicity tends toward God; purity apprehends and tastes Him.

No good action will hinder you, if you be inwardly free from inordinate affection. If you intend and seek nothing else but the will of God and the good of your neighbor, you shall thoroughly enjoy inward liberty.

If your heart were right, then every creature would be a mirror of life and a book of holy doctrine. There is no creature so small and mean, that it does not set forth the goodness of God (Rom. 1:20). If you were inwardly good and pure (Prov. 3:3, 4; Ps. 119:100),

69

then you would be able to see and understand all things well without hindrance. A pure heart penetrates Heaven and Hell.

Such as everyone is inwardly, so he judges outwardly. If there is joy in the world, surely a man of pure heart possesses it. And if there be anywhere tribulation and affliction, an evil conscience best knows it.

As iron put into the fire loses its rust, and becomes altogether white and glowing, so he who wholly turns himself unto God, puts off all slothfulness and is transformed into a new man. When a man begins to grow lukewarm, then he is afraid of small labor, and willingly receives outward comfort. But when he once begins to overcome himself perfectly, and to walk manfully in the way of God, then he esteems those things less, which before were grievous unto him.

Chapter 5

CONSIDERATION OF ONESELF

WE CANNOT TRUST overmuch to ourselves (Jer. 17:5), because often grace is lacking in us, and understanding also.

There is little light in us, and this we quickly lose by our negligence. Oftentimes too we perceive not how great is our inward blindness. Oftentimes we do evil, and excuse it. We are sometimes moved with passion, and we think it zeal. We reprehend small things in others, and pass over our own greater matters (Matt. 7:5). Quickly enough we feel and weigh what we suffer at the hands of others; but we mind not how much others suffer from us. He who rightly considers his own works will find little cause to judge another.

The inward Christian prefers the care of himself before all other cares (Matt. 16:26). And he who diligently attends unto himself easily keeps silence concerning others. You will never be thus inwardly devout, unless you be silent concerning other men's matters, and look especially to yourself. If you attend wholly unto yourself and God, you will be little moved with what you see abroad (I Cor. 4:3; Gal. 1:10).

Where are you, when you are not with yourself? And when you have run all over, what have you then profited if you have neglected yourself? If you desire peace of mind and true unity of purpose, you must still put all things behind you, and look only upon yourself. You shall then make great progress, if you keep yourself at leisure from all temporal care. You shall fall back if you esteem anything temporal.

Let nothing be great unto you, nothing high, nothing pleasing, nothing acceptable, except it be simply God, or comes of God. Esteem all comfort vain (Eccles. 1:14), which comes to you from any creature. A soul that loves God, despises all things that are inferior unto God. God alone is everlasting, and of infinite greatness, filling all things, the soul's solace, and the true joy of the heart.

Chapter 6

THE JOY OF A GOOD CONSCIENCE

THE GLORY OF A GOOD MAN is the testimony of a good conscience (I Cor. 1:31).

Have a good conscience, and you shall ever have joy. A good conscience is able to bear much, and is very joyful in adversities. An evil conscience is always fearful and restless.

You shall rest sweetly if your heart does not blame you. Never rejoice, except when you have done well. Sinners have never true joy, nor feel inward peace; because "there is no peace, saith the Lord, unto the wicked" (Isa. 48:22). And if they should say, We are in peace, no evil shall fall upon us (Luke 12:19), and who shall dare to hurt us? believe them not; for suddenly the wrath of God will arise and their deeds shall be brought to nought, and their thoughts shall perish.

To glory in tribulation is no hard thing for him who loves; for to so glory is to glory in the cross of the Lord (Gal. 6:14). Brief is the glory which is given and received from men (John 5:44). The world's glory is ever accompanied by sorrow.

The glory of the good is in their consciences and not in the tongues of men. The gladness of the just is of God (II Cor. 3:5) and in God; and their joy is of the truth. He who desires true and everlasting glory cares not for that which is temporal. And he who seeks temporal glory, or removes it not from his soul, shows that he little loves the glory of Heaven.

He has great tranquility of heart who cares neither for the praises nor the fault-finding of men. He will easily be content and pacified, whose conscience is pure. You are not holier if you are praised; nor the more worthless if you are found fault with. What you are, that you are; neither by words can you be made greater than what you are in the sight of God.

If you consider what you are within, you will not care what men say of you. Man looks on the countenance, but God on the heart (I Sam. 16:7). Man considers the deeds, but God weighs the intentions.

To be always doing well, and to esteem oneself lightly, is the sign of a humble soul. To refuse to be comforted by any creature is a sign of great purity and inward confidence. He who seeks no witness for himself from without shows that he has wholly committed himself unto God. "For not he that commendeth himself is approved, but whom the Lord commendeth" (II Cor. 10:18).

To walk inwardly with God, and not to be kept abroad by any affection, is the state of an inwardly Christian man.

Chapter 7

THE LOVE OF JESUS ABOVE
ALL THINGS

BLESSED IS HE who understands (Ps. 119:1, 2) what it is to love Jesus, and to despise himself for Jesus' sake. You ought to leave your beloved for your Beloved (Deut. 6:5; Matt. 22:37; Song of Sol. 2:16); for Jesus will be loved above all things. The love of things created is deceitful and inconstant; the love of Jesus is faithful and persevering. He who cleaves unto a creature shall fall with that which is subject to fall; he who embraces Jesus shall be made strong forever.

Love Him, and keep Him for your friend, who, when all go away, will not forsake you, nor suffer you to perish in the end. Sometime or other you must be separated from all, whether you will or no. Keep close to Jesus both in life and in death, and commit yourself unto His faithfulness, who, when all fail, can alone help you.

Your Beloved is of that nature that He will admit of no rival, but will have your heart alone, and sit on His throne as King. If you could empty yourself perfectly from all creatures, Jesus would willingly dwell with you.

Whatever you repose in men, out of Jesus, you shall

find almost wholly lost. Trust not nor lean upon a reed shaken by the wind (Matt. 11:7); for that "all flesh is grass, and all the goodliness thereof is as the flower of the field" (Isa. 40:6).

You shall quickly be deceived, if you only look to the outward appearance of men. For if in others you seek your comfort and profit, you shall too often feel loss. If you seek in all things Jesus, you shall surely find Jesus. But if you seek yourself, you shall also find yourself, but to your own destruction. For man is more hurtful to himself if he seek not Jesus, than the whole world and all its adversaries.

Chapter 8

FAMILIAR CONVERSE WITH JESUS

WHEN JESUS IS PRESENT, all is good and nothing seems difficult; but when Jesus is absent, all is hard.

When Jesus speaks not inwardly to us, all other comfort is worth nothing; but if Jesus speak but one word we feel great comfort. Did not Mary rise immediately from the place where she wept, when Martha said to her: "The Master is come, and calleth for thee" (John 11:28)? Happy hour, when Jesus calls from tears to spiritual joy!

How dry and hard are you without Jesus! How foolish and vain, if you desire anything out of Jesus! Is not this a greater loss, than if you should lose the whole world (Matt. 16:26)? What can the world profit you without Jesus? To be without Jesus is a grievous Hell; and to be with Jesus, a sweet Paradise. If Jesus is with you (Rom. 8:35), no enemy shall be able to hurt you. He who finds Jesus finds a good treasure (Matt. 13:44), yea, a Good above all good. And he who loses Jesus loses much indeed, yea, more than the whole world! Poor is he who lives without Jesus (Luke 12:21); and rich is he who is well with Jesus.

It is great skill to know how to hold converse with Jesus; and to know how to keep Jesus, great wisdom. Be humble and peaceable, and Jesus will be with you (Prov. 3:17). Be devout and quiet, and Jesus will stay with you.

You may soon drive away Jesus, and lose His favor if you turn aside to outward things. And if you should drive Him from you and lose Him, unto whom will you go, and whom will you then seek for your friend? Without a friend you cannot live well, and if Jesus is not above all a Friend to you, you shall be indeed sad and desolate. You act therefore like an idiot, if you trust or rejoice in any other (Gal. 6:14). It is preferable to have all the world against us, rather than to have Jesus offended with us. Among all therefore that be dear unto us, let Jesus alone be specially beloved.

Love all for Jesus, but Jesus for Himself. Jesus Christ alone is singularly to be beloved. He alone is found good and faithful above all friends. For Him. and in Him, let both friends and foes be dear unto you.

And all these are to be prayed for, that He would make them all to know and love Him (Matt. 5:44; Luke 6:27, 28).

Never desire to be singularly commended or beloved, for that appertains only unto God, who hath none like unto Himself. Neither desire that the heart of any should be set on you, nor set your heart on the love of any; but let Jesus be in you, and in every good man.

Be pure and free within, and not entangled with any creature. You ought to carry your heart pure toward God, if you would be free from the world and see how good the Lord is (Ps. 34:8). And truly, unless you be prevented and drawn by His grace, you shall never attain to that happiness, to empty yourself of all, and take leave of all, that you alone may with Him alone be made one. For when the grace of God comes unto a man, then he is made able for all things. And when it goes away, then shall he be poor and weak, and, as it were, left only to stripes. In this case he ought not to be cast down, nor to despair, but at God's will to stand with even mind, and whatever come upon him to endure it for the glory of Jesus Christ. For after winter follows summer, after night the day returns, and after a tempest a great calm (Matt. 8:26).

Chapter 9

WANT OF ALL COMFORT

IT IS NO HARD MATTER to despise human comfort when we have divine. It is a great thing, yea, very great, to be able to want both human and divine comfort; and, for God's honor, to be willing cheerfully to endure the heart's banishment, and to seek oneself in nothing, nor to regard one's own merit.

What does it matter if at the coming of grace you are cheerful and devout? This hour is wished for by all men. Sweetly enough he rides whom the grace of God carries. And what marvel if he feel not his burden, who is borne up by the Almighty, and led by the Sovereign Guide?

We are always willing to have something for our comfort; and a man strips himself of self with difficulty.

Learn to leave even a near and dear friend for the love of God. Do not take it hard when you are deserted by a friend, as knowing that we all at last must be separated one from another.

A man must strive much and long within himself, before he can learn fully to master himself, and to draw his whole affection unto God. When a man stands on himself, he easily slides into human comforts. But a true lover of Christ, and a diligent follower of virtues, does not fall back on comforts, or seek such sensible sweetnesses; but rather seeks hard exercises, and to bear severe labors for Christ.

When therefore spiritual comfort is given from God receive it with thanksgiving; but understand that it is the gift of God, not your merit. Be not puffed up, be not too joyful or vainly presumptuous; but rather be the more humble for that gift, more wary too and fearful in all your actions; for that hour will pass away and temptation will follow. When consolation is taken from you, do not immediately despair; but with humility and patience wait for the heavenly visitation; for God is able to give ample consolation.

This is nothing new nor strange unto them who have experience in the way of God; for the great saints and ancient prophets oftentimes had experiences of such vicissitudes. For which cause, one, while grace was present with him, said: "In my prosperity, I said, I shall never be moved" (Ps. 30:6-11). But when this grace was absent, what he found in himself he goes on to speak of, saying: "Thou didst hide thy face, and I was troubled." Yet in the midst of all this he does not despair, but more earnestly beseeches the Lord: "I cried to thee, O Lord: and unto the Lord I made supplication." At length he receives the fruit of his prayer, and testifies that he was heard, saying: "Hear, O Lord, and have mercy upon me: Lord, be thou my helper. Thou hast turned for me my mourning into dancing . . . and girded me with gladness." If great saints were so dealt with, we who are weak and poor ought not to despair if we are sometimes fervent and sometimes cold; for the Spirit comes and goes, according to the good pleasure of His own will (John 3:8). For which cause Job saith: "That thou shouldest visit him every morning and try him every moment" (Job 7:18).

Whereupon then can I hope, or wherein ought I to trust, save in the great mercy of God alone, and in the hope alone of heavenly grace? For whether I have with me good men, or religious brethren and faithful friends; whether holy books or fair treatises, or sweet chanting and hymns, all these help but little, and have but little savor, when I am forsaken of grace and left in my own poverty. At such time there is no better remedy than patience, and the denial of myself according to the will of God (Luke 9:23).

I have never found man so religious and devout that he had not sometimes a withdrawing of grace, or felt not some decrease of zeal. There was never a saint so high caught up (II Cor. 12:2) and illuminated, who first or last was not tempted. For he is not worthy of the high contemplation of God, who has not been exercised with some tribulation for God's sake. Temptation going before is wont to be a sign of ensuing comfort. For unto those who are proved by temptations, heavenly comfort is promised. "To him that overcometh will I give to eat of the tree of life" (Rev. 2:7). But divine consolation is given that a man may be bolder to bear adversities. There follows also temptation, lest he should wax proud of any good. The Devil sleeps not (I Peter 5:8), neither is the flesh as yet dead. Therefore cease not to prepare yourself to the battle, for on your right hand and on your left are enemies who never rest.

Chapter 10

GRATITUDE FOR THE GRACE OF GOD

WHY SEEK REST, since you are born to trouble (Job 5:7)? Dispose yourself to patience rather than to comfort, and to the bearing of the cross rather than to gladness (Luke 14:27).

What secular person is there who would not willingly receive comfort and spiritual joy, if he could always have it? For spiritual comforts exceed all the delights of the world and pleasures of the flesh. For all worldly delights are either vain or unclean; but spiritual delights are only pleasant and honest, sprung from virtues, and infused by God into pure minds.

But these divine comforts can no man always enjoy according to his desire; for the time of temptation ceases not.

But false freedom of mind and great confidence of ourselves is very contrary to the heavenly visitation.

God does well for us in giving the grace of comfort; but man does evil in not returning all again unto God with thanksgiving. And therefore the gifts of grace cannot flow in us, because we are unthankful to the Giver, and do not return them wholly to the Head-fountain. For grace ever attends him who duly gives thanks; and from the proud shall be taken that which is wont to be given to the humble.

I desire not that consolation which takes from me contrition; nor do I aim at that contemplation which leads to haughtiness of mind. For not all that is high is holy; nor all that is sweet, good; nor every desire, pure; nor is everything that is dear unto us pleasing to God. Willingly do I accept of that grace, whereby I may ever be found humbler, and more fearful, and may become readier to renounce myself.

He who is taught by the gift of grace, and schooled by the rod of its withdrawing, will not dare to attribute any good to himself, but will rather acknowledge himself poor and naked. Give unto God that which is God's (Matt. 22:21) and ascribe unto yourself that which is your own; that is, give thanks to God for His grace, and feel that to yourself alone the fault, and the fit punishment of the fault, are due.

Set yourself always in the lowest place (Luke 14: 10) and the highest shall be given you; for the highest cannot stand without the lowest. The chiefest saints before God are the least before themselves, and the more glorious they are, so much within themselves are they humbler. Those who are full of truth and heavenly glory are not greedy of vainglory. Those who are firmly settled and grounded in God can no wise be puffed up. And they who ascribe all unto God, whatever good they have received, seek not glory one of another, but wish for that glory which is from God alone and desire above all things that God may be praised in them, and in all His saints; and after this very thing they are always striving.

Be therefore thankful for the least gift and you shall be ready to receive greater. Let the least be even as the greatest, yea, the most contemptible gift as of special value. If you consider the worth of the Giver, no gift will seem little, or of too small esteem. For that cannot be little which is given by the Most High God. Yea, if He should give punishment and stripes, it ought to be a matter of thankfulness because He does it always for our welfare, whatever He permits to happen to us.

He who desires to keep the grace of God, let him be thankful for grace given, and patient for the taking away thereof. Let him pray that it may return; let him be cautious and humble, lest he lose it.

Chapter 11

LOVERS OF THE CROSS OF JESUS

JESUS HAS NOW many lovers of His heavenly kingdom, but few bearers of His cross. Many He has who are desirous of consolation, but few of tribulation. Many He finds who share His table, but few His fasting. All desire to rejoice with Him, few are willing to endure anything for Him. Many follow Jesus unto the breaking of bread; but few to the drinking of the cup of His passion (Luke 22:42). Many reverence His miracles; few follow the shame of His cross. Many love Jesus so long as no adversities befall them. Many praise and bless Him, so long as they receive any consolation from Him. But if Jesus hide Himself, and leave them but a little while, they fall either into complaining, or into dejection of mind.

But they who love Jesus for the sake of Jesus, and not for some special comfort of their own, bless Him in all tribulation and anguish of heart, as well as in the highest comfort. Yea, although He should never give them comfort, they would ever praise Him notwithstanding, and wish to always give thanks. Oh, how powerful is the pure love of Jesus, which is mixed with no self-interest, or self-love!

Are not all those to be called hirelings, who are ever seeking consolations? Do they not show themselves to be rather lovers of themselves than of Christ, who are always thinking of their own advantage and profit (Phil. 2:21)?

Where shall one be found who is willing to serve God for nought (Job 1:9)? Rarely is anyone found so spiritual as to be stripped of all things. For who shall find one who is indeed poor in spirit and stripped of every created thing? "Her price is far above rubies" (Prov. 31:10).

"If a man would give all [his] substance," yet it is nothing (Song of Sol. 8:7). And if he should practice great repentance, still it is little. And if he should attain to all knowledge, still he is afar off. And if he should have great virtue and very fervent devotion, yet there is much wanting to him; especially one thing, which is for him most chiefly necessary. What is that? That, forsaking all, he forsake himself, and go forth wholly from himself (Matt. 16:24) and retain nothing of self-love. And when he has done all that he knows ought to be done, let him think that he has done nothing. Let him not weigh that much, which might be much esteemed; but let him pronounce himself to be in truth an unprofitable servant. "When ye shall have done all those things which are commanded you, say, We are unprofitable servants" (Luke 17:10).

Then may he be truly poor and naked in spirit, and say with the psalmist: "I am desolate and afflicted" (Ps. 25:16). Yet no man richer than he, no man more powerful, no man more free: for he is able to leave himself and all things, and to set himself in the lowest place.

Chapter 12

THE KING'S HIGHWAY OF THE HOLY CROSS

To many this seems a hard saying, Deny thyself, take up thy cross, and follow Jesus (Matt. 16:24). But it will be much harder to hear that last word: "Depart from me, ye cursed, into everlasting fire" (Matt. 25:41). For they who now willingly hear and follow the word of the cross shall not then fear (Ps. 112:7) to hear the sentence of everlasting damnation. This sign of the Son of man shall be in Heaven when the Lord shall come to judgment (Matt. 24:30). Then all the servants of the cross, who in their lifetime conformed themselves unto Christ crucified, shall draw near unto Christ the Judge with great confidence. Why therefore fear to take up the cross which leads to a kingdom?

In the cross is salvation, in the cross is life, in the cross is protection against our enemies, in the cross is infusion of heavenly sweetness, in the cross is strength of mind, in the cross joy of spirit, in the cross the height of virtue, in the cross the perfection of holiness. There is no salvation of the soul, or hope of everlasting life, but in the cross. Take up therefore your cross and follow Jesus (Luke 14:27), and you shall go into life everlasting. He went before, bearing His cross (John 19:17), and died for you on the cross; that you also may bear your cross and desire to die on the cross. For if you be dead with Him, you shall also in like manner live with Him (Gal. 2:20; Rom. 6:8). And if you share His punishment, you shall also share His glory (II Cor. 1:5).

Behold, in the cross all consists, and in our dying thereon all lies! For there is no other way unto life, and unto true inward peace, but the way of the cross and of daily mortification. Walk where you will, seek whatever you will, you shall not find a higher way above, nor a safer way below, than the way of the cross.

Dispose and order all things according to your will and judgment, and you shall find that you must always suffer somewhat, either willingly or against your will, and so you shall ever find the cross. For either you shall feel pain in the body, or suffer tribulation of spirit in the soul. Sometimes you shall be forsaken of God, sometimes you shall be troubled by your neighbor; and, what is more, oftentimes you shall be wearisome to your own self. Neither can you be delivered or eased by any remedy or comfort; but so long as it pleases God you ought to bear it. For God will have you learn to suffer tribulation without comfort; and that you subject yourself wholly to Him, and by tribulation become more humble. No man so feels in his heart the passion of Christ as he who suffers.

The cross therefore is always ready, and everywhere waits for you. You cannot escape it wherever you run; for wherever you go you carry yourself with you, and shall ever find yourself. Turn above, turn below, turn without, turn within, and in all these places you shall find the cross. And everywhere of necessity you must hold fast patience if you will have inward peace, and win an everlasting crown.

If you bear the cross cheerfully, it will bear you, and lead you to the desired end, to where there shall be an end of suffering; though this shall not be here. If you bear it unwillingly, you make for yourself a load, and burden yourself the more, and yet notwithstanding you must bear it. If you cast away one cross, without doubt you shall find another, and perhaps a heavier one.

Do you think you can escape that which no mortal man could ever avoid? Which of the saints in the world was without cross and tribulation? For not even our Lord Jesus Christ was ever one hour without the anguish of His passion, so long as He lived. "Ought not Christ to have suffered these things, and to enter into his glory" (Luke 24:26). And why do you seek any other way than this royal way, which is the way of the cross? The whole life of Christ was a cross and martyrdom; and do you seek rest and joy for yourself? You are deceived if you seek any other thing than to suffer tribulations; for the whole of this mortal life is full of miseries (Job 7:1), and signed on every side with crosses. And the higher a person has advanced in the Spirit, the heavier the crosses he oftentimes finds, because the grief of his banishment increases with his love.

Nevertheless, this man, though so many ways afflicted, is not without refreshing comfort, for he perceives much fruit by the enduring of his own cross. For while he willingly puts himself under it, all the burden of tribulation is turned into the confidence of divine comfort. And the more the flesh is wasted in affliction, the more is the spirit made strong by inward grace (II Cor. 4:16). And sometimes he is so strengthened by the desire of tribulation and adversity, for the love of conformity to the cross of Christ, that he would not wish to be without pain and tribulation (II Cor. 11:23-30). He believes that he shall be unto God so much the more acceptable, the more and the heavier things he can suffer for Him.

This is not the power of man, but it is the grace of Christ, which does so much in frail flesh; so that what naturally it always abhors and flees from, this by fervor of spirit it encounters and loves. It is not according to man to bear the cross, to love the cross, to mortify the body, and bring it into subjection, to flee honors, willingly to suffer reproaches, to despise himself and wish to be despised, to endure all adversities and losses, and to desire no prosperity in this world. If you look to yourself, nothing of this kind shall you be able of yourself to accomplish (II Cor. 3:5). But if you trust in the Lord, fortitude shall be given from Heaven, and the world and the flesh shall be made subject to your sway. Neither shall you fear your Enemy, the Devil, if you are armed with faith, and signed with the cross of Christ.

Set yourself therefore, like a good and faithful servant of Christ, to bear manfully the cross of your Lord, who out of love for you was crucified. Prepare yourself to bear many adversities and divers troubles in this miserable life; for so it will be with you, wherever you are, and so surely you shall find it wherever you hide yourself. So it must be; nor is there any remedy or means to escape from tribulation and pain of evils, but only to endure. Drink of the Lord's cup (Matt. 20: 23) with all your heart, if you desire to be His friend, and to have part with Him. As for comforts, leave them to God; let Him do as shall best please Him. But set yourself to suffer tribulations, and account them the greatest comforts: "For the sufferings of this present time," although you alone could suffer them all, "are not worthy to be compared with the glory which shall be revealed in us" (Rom. 8:18).

When you shall come to this state—that tribulation (Rom. 5:3; Gal. 6:14) shall seem sweet, and you shall relish it for Christ's sake—then think it to be well with you, for you have found Heaven upon earth. As long as it is grievous to you to suffer, and you desire to flee it, so long shall you be ill at ease, and the desire of escaping tribulation will follow you everywhere. If you set yourself to what you ought, namely, to suffering and to death, it will be better with you and you shall find peace.

Although you were caught up even unto the third heaven with Paul (II Cor. 12:4), you are not secure from suffering adversity. "I will show him," saith Jesus, "how great things he must suffer for my name's sake" (Acts 9:16). To suffer, therefore, remains if you love Jesus and serve Him perpetually. Oh, that you were worthy to suffer something for the name of Jesus (Acts 5:41)! How great glory would remain for you; what joy would arise to all God's saints; how great edification also to your neighbor! For all men recommend patience; few, however, are they who are willing to suffer. With great reason ought you cheerfully to suffer a little for Christ, since many suffer more grievous things for the world.

Know for certain that you ought to lead a dying life (Ps. 44:22). And the more any man dies to himself, so much the more he begins to live unto God. No man is fit to comprehend things heavenly, unless he submit himself to the bearing of adversities for Christ's sake. Nothing is more acceptable to God, nothing more wholesome to you in this world, than to suffer cheerfully for Christ. And if it were for you to choose, you ought rather to suffer adversities for Christ, than to be refreshed with many consolations; because you would thus be more like unto Christ. For our worthiness, and the progress of our spiritual state, stands not in many sweetnesses and comforts, but rather in thoroughly enduring great afflictions and tribulations.

Indeed, if there had been any better thing, and more profitable to a man's salvation, than suffering, surely Christ would have shown it by word and example. For both the disciples who followed Him, and all who desire to follow Him, He plainly exhorts to the bearing of the cross, and saith: "If any man will come after me, let him deny himself, and take up his cross daily, and follow me" (Luke 9:23). So when we have read to the end and searched through all, let this be the final conclusion: "That we must through much tribulation enter into the kingdom of God" (Acts 14:22).

The Third Book

INTERNAL CONSOLATION

Chapter 1

CHRIST SPEAKS TO THE FAITHFUL

I WILL HEAR what God the Lord will speak" (Ps. 85:8). Blessed is the soul which hears the Lord speaking within, and from His mouth receives the word of consolation. Blessed are the ears that catch the pulses of the divine whisper (Matt. 13:16, 17), and give no heed to the whisperings of this world. Blessed indeed are those ears which listen not after the voice which is sounding without, but for the truth teaching inwardly. Blessed are the eyes that are shut to outward things, but intent on things inward. Blessed are they that enter far into things within, and endeavor to prepare themselves more and more, by daily exercises, for the receiving of heavenly secrets. Blessed are they who are glad to have time to spare for God, and who shake off all worldly hindrances.

Consider these things, O my soul, and shut up the door of your sensual desires, that you may hear what the Lord your God speaks in you (Ps. 85:8).

Thus says your Beloved, "I am thy salvation," your Peace, and your Life: keep yourself with Me, and you shall find peace. Let go all transitory things, and seek the things eternal. What are all transitory objects but seductive things? And what can all creatures avail, if you are forsaken by the Creator?

Renounce therefore all things, and labor to please your Creator, and to be faithful unto Him, that you may be able to attain unto true blessedness.

Chapter 2

THE TRUTH SPEAKS INWARDLY

SPEAK, LORD, for thy servant heareth" (I Sam. 3:9). "I am thy servant; give me understanding, that I may know thy testimonies (Ps. 119:125). "Hear, O earth, the words of my mouth . . . my speech shall distil as the dew" (Deut. 32:1, 2).

The children of Israel in times past said unto Moses: "Speak thou with us, and we will hear: but let not God speak with us, lest we die" (Exod. 20:19). Not so, Lord, not so, I beseech Thee: but rather with the prophet Samuel, I humbly and earnestly entreat: "Speak, Lord, for thy servant heareth."

Let not Moses speak unto me, nor any of the prophets, but rather do Thou speak, O Lord God, the Inspirer and Enlightener of all the prophets; for Thou alone without them canst perfectly instruct me, but they without Thee will profit nothing.

They may indeed sound forth words, but they cannot give the Spirit. Beautiful is their speech, but if

Thou be silent, they kindle not the heart. They give the letter, but Thou openest the sense; they bring forth mysteries, but Thou unlockest the meaning of things that are sealed. They declare commandments, but Thou helpest us to fulfill them. They point out the way, but Thou givest strength to walk in it. They work only from without, but Thou instructest and enlightenest hearts. They water outwardly, but Thou givest the increase (I Cor. 3:6). They cry aloud in words, but Thou to the hearing impartest understanding.

Let not Moses therefore speak unto me, but Thou, O Lord my God, the Everlasting Truth; lest haply I die, and prove unfruitful, if I be only warned outwardly, and not set on fire within, lest it turn to my condemnation—the word heard and not fulfilled, known and not loved, believed and not kept. Speak therefore, Lord, for Thy servant heareth; for "thou hast the words of eternal life" (John 6:68). Speak Thou unto me, to the comfort, however imperfect, of my soul, and to the amendment of my whole life, and to Thy praise and glory and honor everlasting.

Chapter 3

THE WORDS OF GOD TO BE
HEARD WITH HUMILITY

M Y SON, hear My words, words of greatest sweetness, surpassing all the knowledge of the philosophers and wise men of this world. My words are spirit and life (John 6:63), and not to be weighed by the understanding of man. They are not to be drawn forth for vain self-pleasing, but to be heard in silence, and to be received with all humility and great affection.

And I said: "Blessed is the man whom thou chastenest, O Lord, and teachest him out of thy law; that thou mayest give him rest from the days of adversity" (Ps. 94:12, 13), and that he be not desolate upon earth.

I, saith the Lord, have taught the prophets from the beginning (Heb. 1:1), and cease not, even to this day, to speak to all; but many are deaf, and hardened to My voice. Most men more willingly listen to the world than to God. They follow the desire of their own flesh rather than God's good pleasure.

The world promises things temporal and mean, and is served with great eagerness. I promise things most high and eternal, and the hearts of mortals grow dull.

Who is there that in all things serves and obeys Me with so great care as the world and its lords are served withal? "Be ashamed, O Zidon: for the sea hath spoken" (Isa. 23:4). And if you ask the cause, hear wherefore. For a small income, a long journey is made; for everlasting life, many scarce once lift a foot from the ground. A pitiful reward is sought after; for a single piece of money sometimes there is shameful strife at law; for a vain matter and a slight promise men fear not to toil day and night. But, ah, shame, for a good that changes not, for a reward that cannot be reckoned, for the highest honor, and glory without end, they grudge even the least fatigue! Be ashamed, therefore, slothful and complaining servant, that they are found more ready to destruction than you to life. They rejoice more in vanity than you in the truth.

Sometimes, indeed, they are disappointed of their hope; but My promise deceives none (Rom. 1:16; Matt. 24:35), nor sends him away empty who trusts in Me. What I have promised, I will give; what I have said, I will fulfill; if only a man remain faithful in My love even to the end. I am the Rewarder of all good men (Rev. 2:23; Matt. 5:6; 25:21), and the strong Approver of all who are devoted to Me.

Write My words in your heart, and meditate diligently on them; for in time of temptation they will be very needful. What you understand not when you read, you shall know in the day of visitation. In two ways I am wont to visit Mine elect, namely, with temptation and with consolation. And I daily read two lessons to them, one in reproving their vices, another in exhorting them to the increase of virtues.

He that hath My words and despiseth them, hath One that "shall judge him in the last day" (John 12:48).

A prayer to implore the grace of devotion.

O Lord, my God! Thou art all my good things. And who am I, that I should dare speak to Thee (Gen. 18:27)? I am Thy poorest, meanest servant, and a vile worm, much poorer and more contemptible than I know or dare express.

Yet do Thou remember me, O Lord, because I am nothing, I have nothing, and I can do nothing. Thou alone art good, just and holy. Thou canst do all things, Thou suppliest all things, Thou fillest all things, only the sinner Thou leavest empty. "Remember, O Lord, thy tender mercies" (Ps. 25:6), and fill my heart with Thy grace, Thou who willest not that Thy works should be void. How can I bear up myself in this miserable life, unless Thou strengthen me with Thy mercy and grace?

"Hide not thy face from thy servant" (Ps. 69:17); delay not Thy visitation; withdraw not Thy consolation, lest my soul become as a thirsty land unto Thee (Ps. 143:6). "Teach me to do thy will" (Ps. 143:10); teach me to live worthily and humbly in Thy sight; for Thou art my wisdom, who dost truly know me, and didst know me before the world was made, and before I was born in the world.

Chapter 4

LIVE IN TRUTH AND HUMILITY
BEFORE GOD

M Y SON, walk thou before Me in truth, and in the simplicity of thine heart seek Me evermore (Gen. 17:1). He that walks before Me in truth shall be defended from evil attacks, and the truth shall set him (John 8:32) free from seducers, and from the slanders of unjust men. "If the Son therefore shall make you free, ye shall be free indeed" (John 8:36), and shall not care for the vain words of men.

O Lord, it is true! According as Thou sayest, so, I beseech Thee, let it be with me; let Thy truth teach me, itself guard me, and preserve me to an end of safety. Let it set me free from all evil affection and inordinate love; and I shall walk with Thee in great liberty of heart.

I will teach thee (saith the Truth) those things which are right and pleasing in My sight.

Reflect on your sins with great displeasure and grief; and never esteem yourself to be anything because of good works.

In truth you are a sinner; you are subject to and entangled with many passions. Of yourself you always tend to nothing; you are quickly cast down, quickly overcome, quickly confused, quickly dissolved. You have nothing whereof you can glory (I Cor. 4:7), but many things for which you ought to account yourself vile; for you are much weaker than you are able to comprehend.

Let nothing therefore seem much of all the things you do. Let nothing seem great, nothing precious and wonderful, nothing worthy of estimation, nothing high, nothing truly commendable and to be desired, but that alone which is eternal. Let the eternal truth be above all things pleasing to you. Let your own extreme unworthiness be always displeasing to you. Fear nothing, blame nothing, flee nothing, so much as your vices and sins, which ought to be more unpleasing to you than any losses whatever of things earthly.

Some walk not sincerely in My sight (II Cor. 2:17), but led by a certain curiosity and arrogance wish to know My secrets, and to understand the deep things of God, neglecting themselves and their own salvation. These oftentimes, when I resist them for their pride and curiosity, fall into great temptations and sins. Fear the judgments of God; dread the wrath of the Almighty. Do not, however, discuss the works of the Most High, but search diligently your own iniquities, in how great things you have offended, and how many good things you have neglected.

Some carry their devotion only in books, some in pictures, some in outward signs and figures. Some have Me often in their mouths; but little of Me in their hearts (Isa. 29:13).

Others there are who, being illuminated in their

understandings, and purged in their affection, always long after things eternal, are unwilling to hear of earthly things, and serve the necessities of nature with grief. And these perceive what the Spirit of truth speaks in them (Ps. 25:5), for He teaches them to despise earthly and to love heavenly things; to neglect the world and to desire Heaven day and night (Ps. 1:2).

Chapter 5

THE WONDERFUL EFFECT OF DIVINE LOVE

I BLESS THEE, O heavenly Father, Father of the Lord Jesus Christ, for that Thou hast vouchsafed to remember me that am poor. "Father of mercies, and the God of all comfort" (II Cor. 1:3), thanks be unto Thee, who sometimes with Thy comfort refreshest me, unworthy as I am of all comfort. I will always bless and glorify Thee, with Thy only begotten Son, and the Holy Ghost, the Comforter, forever and ever. Ah, Lord God, Thou Holy One who lovest me; when Thou comest into my heart, all that is within me shall rejoice. Thou art my glory and the exultation of my heart; Thou art my Hope and "refuge in the day of my trouble" (Ps. 32:7; 59:16).

But because I am as yet weak in love, and imperfect

in virtue, I have need to be strengthened and comforted by Thee. Visit me therefore often, and instruct me with all holy discipline. Set me free from evil passions, and heal my heart of all inordinate affections; that being inwardly healed and thoroughly cleansed, I may be made ready to love, strong to suffer, steady to persevere.

Love is a great thing, yea, altogether a great good; it makes light everything that is heavy, and it bears evenly all that is uneven. For it carries a burden which is no burden (Matt. 11:30), and makes every bitter thing sweet and tasteful. The noble love of Jesus drives a man to do great things, and stirs him to always long for what is more perfect. Love wills to be on high, and not to be kept back by anything low and mean. Love wills to be free, and estranged from all worldly affection, so its inward sight may not be hindered; that it may not be entangled by any temporal prosperity, or by any adversity subdued.

Nothing is sweeter than love, nothing stronger, nothing higher, nothing wider, nothing more pleasant, nothing fuller or better in Heaven and earth; because love is born of God (I John 4:7) and cannot rest but in God, above all created things. A lover flies, runs, and rejoices; he is free and is not bound. He gives all for all, and has all in all; because he rests in One highest above all things, from whom all that is good flows. He respects not the gifts, but turns himself above all goods unto the Giver.

Love oftentimes knows no measure, but is fervent beyond all measure. Love feels no burden, thinks nothing of labors, attempts what is above its strength, pleads no excuse of impossibility; for it thinks all things possible for itself and all things lawful. It is therefore strong for all things, and it completes many things, and brings them to effect, where he who does not love faints and lies down. Love is watchful, and sleeping slumbers not. Though wearied, it is not tired; though pressed, it is not straitened; though alarmed, it is not confounded; but as a lively flame and burning torch, it forces its way upward and securely passes through all. If any man love, he knows what is the cry of this voice. For it is a loud cry in the ears of God, that ardent affection of the soul, when it says: "My God, object of my love, Thou art all mine, and I am all Thine."

Enlarge me in love, that with the inward palate of my heart I may learn to taste how sweet it is to love, and in love to be dissolved and to bathe myself. Let me be bound by love, mounting above myself, through excessive fervor and wonder. Let me sing the song of love, let me follow Thee, my Beloved, on high; let my soul spend itself in Thy praise, rejoicing through love. Let me love Thee more than myself, nor love myself but for Thee; and in Thee all that truly love Thee, as the law of love commands, shining out from Thyself.

Love is swift, sincere, kindly affectioned, pleasant and delightsome; brave, patient, faithful, prudent, longsuffering, manly, and never seeking itself (I Cor. 13:5). For where a person seeks himself, there he falls from love (I Cor. 10:33; Phil. 2:21).

Love is circumspect, humble, and upright; not

yielding to softness, or to lightness, nor attending to vain things. It is sober, chaste, firm, quiet, and guarded in all the senses.

Love is subject and obedient to its superiors, to itself mean and despised, unto God devout and thankful, trusting and hoping always in Him, even when God is not sweet unto it: for without sorrow none lives in love. He that is not prepared to suffer all things, and to do the will of his Beloved, is not worthy to be called a lover (Rom. 8:35). A lover ought to embrace willingly all that is hard and bitter, for the sake of his Beloved; nor to turn away from Him for things that fall out against one.

Chapter 6

PROVING A TRUE LOVER

My son, you are not yet a valiant and wise lover. Wherefore, O Lord?

Because for a slight opposition you fail from your undertakings, and too eagerly seek consolation. A valiant lover stands firm in temptations, and gives no credit to the crafty persuasions of the enemy. As I please him in prosperity, so in adversity I displease him not (Phil. 4:11-13). A wise lover regards not so much the gift of Him who loves, as the love of Him who gives. He esteems affection rather than value,

106

and sets all gifts below the Beloved. A noble-minded lover rests not in the gift, but in Me above every gift.

All is not therefore lost, if sometimes you have less feeling for Me than you would. That good and sweet affection which you sometimes feel is the effect of grace present, and a sort of foretaste of your native land of Heaven; but hereon you must not lean too much, for it comes and goes. But to strive against evil motions of the mind, and to reject (Matt. 4:10) with scorn a suggestion of the Devil is a notable sign of virtue and shall have great reward.

Let not strange fancies therefore trouble you, on whatever matter they may be, which are forced into your mind. Bravely keep your purpose, and an upright intention toward God. Neither is it an illusion that sometimes you are suddenly rapt into ecstasy, and presently return again to the wonted follies of your heart. For these you rather unwillingly suffer, than commit; and so long as they displease you, and you strive against them, it is a matter of reward and no loss.

Know that the ancient Enemy strives by all means to hinder your desire to do good, and to keep you void of all religious exercises; particularly from the devout remembrance of My passion, from the profitable calling to mind of sins, from the guard of your own heart, and from the firm purpose of advancing in virtue. Many evil thoughts he forces on you, that he may cause a weariness and horror, to call you back from prayer and holy reading. Humble confession is displeasing to him; and if he could, he would cause you to cease from holy communion.

Believe him not, nor regard him, although he often sets snares of deceit. Charge him with it when he suggests evil and unclean thoughts. Say to him, "Away you unclean spirit" (Matt. 16:23)! Blush, you miserable wretch! Most unclean are you that bring such things to my ears. Begone from me, you wicked Seducer! You shall have no part in me, but Jesus shall be with me as a strong Warrior, and you shall stand confounded. I had rather die, and undergo any torment, than consent to you. Hold your peace and be dumb; I will hear you no more, though you work me many troubles. "The Lord is my light and my salvation; whom shall I fear? . . . Though an host should encamp against me, my heart shall not fear" (Ps. 27:1,3).

Fight like a good soldier (I Tim. 6:12). And if you sometimes fall through frailty, take again strength greater than the former, trusting in My more abundant grace, and take great heed against vain pleasing of yourself, and pride. Through this are many led into error, and sometimes fall into blindness almost incurable. Let this fall of the proud, presuming foolishly of themselves, serve as a warning, and keep you ever humble.

Chapter 7

CONCEAL GRACE UNDER THE GUARD OF HUMILITY

IT IS MORE PROFITABLE for you and safer to conceal the grace of devotion; not to lift yourself on high, nor to speak much thereof, or to dwell much thereon; but rather to despise yourself, and to fear this grace, as given to one unworthy of it.

This disposition must not be too earnestly held to, for it may be quickly changed to the contrary. When you are in grace, think how miserable and needy you would be without grace.

Nor is it in this only that your progress in spiritual life consists, when you have the grace of comfort. But rather when with humility, self-denial, and patience, you endure the withdrawing thereof; provided you do not then become listless in the zeal of prayer, nor neglect the rest of your accustomed duties. But cheerfully perform what lies in you, according to the best of your power and understanding; and do not, because of the dryness or anxiety of mind which you feel, wholly neglect yourself. For there are many who become impatient or slothful. For the way of man is not always in his power (Jer. 10:23; Rom. 9:16), but it belongs to God to give, and to comfort, when He will, and how much He will, and whom He will; as it shall please Him, and no more.

Some unadvised persons, to gain the grace of devotion, have overdone; because they attempted more than they were able to perform, not weighing the measure of their own littleness, but rather following the desire of their hearts than the judgment of their reason. And because they presumed on greater matters than was pleasing to God, they therefore quickly lost His grace. They who had set their nests (Obad. 4) in Heaven were made helpless and vile outcasts; to the end that being humbled and made poor, they might learn not to fly with their own wings, but to trust under My wings (Ps. 91:4).

They that are novices and inexperienced in the way of the Lord, unless they govern themselves by the counsel of discreet persons, may easily be deceived and broken to pieces. And if they will rather follow their own feelings than trust to others who are more experienced, their end will be dangerous, at least if they are unwilling to be drawn back from their own fond conceit. It is seldom the case that they who are self-wise endure humbly to be governed by others. Better it is to have a small portion of good sense with humility (Ps. 16:2; 17:10), and little understanding, than great treasures of many sciences with vain self-pleasing. Better it is to have little, than much of that which may make you proud.

He acts indiscreetly, who wholly gives himself over to joy, forgetting his former poverty, and that chastened fear of the Lord, which is afraid of losing the grace which has been offered. Nor again is he very wise who, in time of adversity or any heaviness, bears himself with too much despondency, and reflects and thinks of Me less confidingly than he ought. He, who in time of peace is willing to be oversecure (I Thess. 5:6) shall be often found in time of war too dejected and full of fears. If you had the wit always to continue humble and moderate within, and also to restrain and govern your spirit, you would not so quickly fall into danger and offense.

It is good counsel, that when a spirit of fervor is kindled within, you should consider how it will be when that light shall leave you. And when this happens, then remember that the light may return again; which, as a warning to yourself and for Mine own glory, I have withdrawn for a time (Job 7). Such a trial is oftentimes more profitable than if you should always have things prosper according to your will. For a man's deserts are not to be reckoned by this, whether he may have many visions and consolations, or be skilled in the Scriptures, or be set in a higher station than others; but whether he be grounded in true humility, and full of divine love; if he be always purely and sincerely seeking God's honor; if he think nothing of and unfeignedly despise himself (Ps. 84: 10), and even rejoice more to be despised and put low by others than to be honored by them.

Chapter 8

A MEAN CONCEIT OF OURSELVES

I HAVE TAKEN upon me to speak unto the Lord, which am but dust and ashes" (Gen. 18:27).

If I esteem myself to be anything more, behold, Thou standest against me, and my iniquities bear true witness, and I cannot contradict it. But if I abase myself, and reduce myself to nothing, and shrink from all self-esteem, and grind myself to (what I am) dust, Thy grace will be favorable to me, and Thy light near unto my heart; and all self-esteem, no matter how little, shall be swallowed up in the valley of my nothingness, and perish forever.

There Thou showest Thyself unto me, what I am, what I have been, and whither I am come; for I am nothing, and I knew it not. If I be left to myself, behold, I am nothing, and altogether weakness! But if Thou for an instant look upon me, I am forthwith made strong and am filled with new joy. And a great marvel it is, that I am so suddenly lifted up, and so graciously embraced by Thee, who of mine own weight am always sinking to the depths.

This is the work of Thy love, freely keeping me, and relieving me in so many necessities, guarding me also from pressing dangers, and snatching me (as I may truly say) from evils without number. For indeed by loving myself amiss, I lost myself (John 12:25); and seeking Thee alone, and purely loving Thee, I have found both myself and Thee; and by that love have more deeply reduced myself to nothing. Because Thou, O sweetest Lord, dealest with me above all desert, and above all that I dare hope for or ask.

Blessed be Thou, my God! For although I am unworthy of any benefits, yet Thy noble bounty and infinite goodness never cease to do good even to the ungrateful (Matt. 5:45), and to those who are turned far away from Thee.

Turn Thou us unto Thee, that we may be thankful, humble, and devout; for Thou art our salvation, our courage, and our strength.

Chapter 9

ALL THINGS TO BE REFERRED UNTO GOD

M Y SON, I ought to be your supreme and ultimate end, if you truly desire to be blessed. With this intention your affections will be purified, which are too often perversely twisted toward self and toward creatures. For if in anything you seek yourself, immediately you faint and dry up within yourself.

Refer all things therefore unto Me in the first place,

for I am He who has given all. Thus think of every-thing as flowing from the highest good; and therefore unto Me as their Spring must all be brought back.

From Me, the small and the great, the poor and the rich draw, as from a living fountain, the water of life (John 4:14); and they that willingly and freely serve Me shall receive "grace for grace" (John 1:16). But he who desires to glory in things outside of Me (I Cor. 1:29), or to take pleasure in some private good, shall not be grounded in true joy, or be enlarged in his heart, but shall in many ways be encumbered and straitened.

Therefore you ought to attribute nothing good to yourself, neither attribute virtue to any man; but give all unto God, without whom man has nothing.

I have given all; I will to have all again; and I require a return of thanks. This is the truth whereby vainglory is put to flight. And if heavenly grace enter in, and true love, there will be no envy or narrowness of heart, neither will self-love have place. For divine love overcomes all things, and enlarges all the powers of the soul.

If you rightly judge, you will rejoice in Me alone, in Me alone you will hope; for "none is good, save one, that is, God" (Matt. 19:17; Luke 18:19), who is above all things to be praised, and in all to be blessed.

Chapter 10

DESPISE THE WORLD AND
SERVE GOD

NOW I WILL SPEAK AGAIN, O Lord, and will not be silent. I will speak in the ears of my God, my Lord, and my King, who is on high.

"Oh how great is thy goodness, which thou hast laid up for them that fear thee" (Ps. 31:19). But what art Thou to those who love Thee? What to those who serve Thee with their whole heart? Truly unspeakable is the sweetness of contemplating Thee, which Thou bestowest on them that love Thee. In this especially Thou hast shown me the sweetness of Thy love—that when I was not, Thou madest me; when I went far astray from Thee, Thou broughtest me back again, that I might serve Thee, and hast commanded me to love Thee (Gen. 1:27; Ps. 119:73; Luke 15).

O Fountain of love unceasing, what shall I say concerning Thee? How can I forget Thee, who hast vouchsafed to remember me, even after I had wasted away and perished? Thou hast shown mercy to Thy servant beyond all hope; and hast exhibited favor and loving-kindness beyond all desert.

What return shall I make to Thee for this grace

(Ps. 116:12)? For it is not granted to all to forsake all, to renounce the world, and to undertake the life of solitude. Is it any great thing that I should serve Thee (Judg. 16:15) whom the whole creation is bound to serve? It ought not to seem much to me to serve Thee. But rather this appears much to me, and wonderful, that Thou vouchsafest to receive into Thy service one so poor and unworthy, and to make him one of Thy beloved servants. Behold, all things are Thine which I have, and whereby I serve Thee (I Cor. 4:7)! And yet contrariwise, Thou servest me rather than I Thee. Behold, Heaven and earth, which Thou hast created for the service of man, are ready at hand, and do daily perform whatever Thou hast commanded! And this is too little; even angels hast Thou appointed to minister to man (Ps. 91:11; Heb. 1:14). But that which excels all this is that Thou Thyself hast vouchsafed to serve man, and hast promised that Thou wouldest give Thyself unto him.

What shall I give Thee for all these thousands of benefits? I would I could serve Thee all the days of my life. I would I were able, at least for one day, to do Thee some worthy service. Truly Thou art worthy of all service, of all honor, and everlasting praise. Truly Thou art my Lord, and I Thy poor servant, who am bound to serve Thee with all my might, neither ought I ever to be disdainful of Thy praises. And this I wish to do, this I desire; and whatever is wanting unto me, do vouchsafe to supply.

It is a great honor and a great glory to serve Thee and to despise all things for Thee. For they shall have

116

great grace, who shall have willingly subjected themselves to Thy most holy service. They shall find the sweetest consolation of the Holy Spirit (Matt. 19:29), who for Thy love have renounced all carnal delight. They shall attain great freedom of mind, who for Thy name's sake enter into the narrow way (Matt. 7:14), and have dropped all worldly care.

O sweet and delightful service of God (Matt. 11:30; I John 5:3), by which a man is made truly free and holy! O sacred state of religious servitude, which makes a man equal to the angels, pleasing to God, terrible to devils, and worthy to be commended of all the unfaithful! O service worthy to be embraced and ever desired, in which the greatest good is offered; and joy is won, which shall endlessly remain!

Chapter 11

OUR HEARTS EXAMINED
AND RULED

M Y SON, it is needful to learn many more things, which you have not yet well learned.

What are these, O Lord?

That you set your longing (Ps. 108:1; Matt. 6:10) wholly according to My good pleasure; and that you be not a lover of yourself, but an earnest follower of My will.

Various longings may often overwhelm you, and drive you forward with vehemence; but consider whether you be moved for My honor, or rather for your own advantage. If I be the cause, you will be well content with whatever I shall ordain. But if there lurk in you any self-seeking (Phil. 2:21), this is it that hinders and weighs you down. Beware therefore you lean not too much upon preconceived desire, without asking My counsel, lest perhaps afterward you regret it; are displeased with that which at first pleased you, and for which you were earnestly zealous, thinking it the best. For not every affection which seems good is immediately to be followed; nor again is every contrary affection at the first to be avoided.

It is sometimes expedient to use a curb, even in good endeavors and longings, lest through importunity you incur distraction of mind; lest by your want of self-government you create a scandal unto others. Or again, being thwarted by others, you become suddenly confounded and fall. Sometimes however you must use violence (Phil. 2:12), and resist manfully your sensual appetite, nor regard what the flesh would or would not (Rom. 8:1-13; II Cor. 4:10; 10:3); but rather for this taking pains, that even perforce it may be made subject to the Spirit (I Cor. 9:27). And so long ought it to be chastised and to be forced to remain under servitude, until it be prepared for all things and learn to be content with little, and to be pleased with simple things, nor to murmur against anything that suits it not.

Chapter 12

THE GROWTH OF PATIENCE
IN THE SOUL

O LORD MY GOD, patience is very necessary for me (Heb. 10:36), as I plainly see, for many things in this life do happen contrary to us. For whatever plans I shall devise for my own peace, my life cannot be without war and pain (Job 7:1).

It is so, My son. But My will is that you seek not that peace which is void of temptation, or which feels nothing contrary. But rather think that you have then found peace, when you are exercised with sundry tribulations (James 1:2), and tried in many crosses.

Do you think that the men of this world suffer nothing, or but a little? Not so shall you find it even if you ask of those who enjoy the greatest delights. But you will say, they have many delights and follow their own wills, and therefore they do not weigh their own afflictions. Be it so, that they do have whatever they will; but how long do you think it will last? Behold, even "as smoke is driven away . . . so let the wicked perish at the presence of God" (Ps. 68:2), and there shall be no memory of their past joys! Yea, even while they are yet alive, they do not rest in them without bitterness, and weariness, and fear. For from the selfsame thing, in which they imagine their delight to be, oftentimes they receive the penalty of sorrow. Justly are they dealt with, because inordinately they seek and follow after delights, they enjoy them not without shame and bitterness. Oh, how brief, how false, how inordinate and filthy, are all those pleasures! Yet so drunken and blind are men that they understand it not; but like dumb beasts, for the poor enjoyment of this corruptible life, they incur the death of the soul.

Therefore, My son, go not after lusts, but refrain from your own will. "Delight thyself also in the Lord; and he shall give thee the desires of thine heart" (Ps. 37:4). For if you desire true delight and to be comforted, behold, in the contempt of all worldly things, and in the cutting off all base delights, shall be your blessing, and abundant consolation shall be rendered to you. And the more you withdraw yourself from all solace of creatures, so much the sweeter and more powerful consolations shall you find in Me.

But at first, you shall not without some sadness, and the toil of conflict, attain unto these. In your way shall stand inbred habit, but by better habit shall it be entirely overcome. The flesh will murmur against you; but with fervency of spirit shall it be bridled. The old Serpent shall sting and irritate you, but by prayer he shall be put to flight. Moreover also, by useful labor shall his approach be barred.

Chapter 13

OBEDIENCE IN HUMBLE SUBJECTION

My son, he who endeavors to withdraw himself from obedience withdraws himself from grace; and he who seeks for himself private benefits (Matt. 16:24) loses those which are common.

He who does not cheerfully and freely submit himself to his superior reveals that his flesh is not as yet perfectly obedient to him, but oftentimes kicks and murmurs against him. Learn therefore quickly to submit yourself to your superior, if you desire to keep your own flesh under the yoke. For more quickly is the outward enemy overcome, if the inward man is not barren. There is no worse nor more troublesome enemy to the soul than you are to yourself, if you be not in harmony with the Spirit. It is altogether necessary that you take up a true contempt for yourself, if you desire to prevail against flesh and blood. Because as yet you love yourself too inordinately; therefore you are afraid to resign yourself wholly to the will of others.

And yet, what great matter is it, if you, who are but dust and nothing, subject yourself to man for God's sake, when I, the Almighty and the Most High, who created all things of nothing, humbly subjected Myself to man for your sake? I became of all men the most humble and the most abject (Luke 2:7; John 13:14), that you might overcome your pride with My humility. O dust, learn to be obedient! Learn to humble yourself, you of earth and clay, and to bow yourself down under the feet of all men. Learn to break your own wishes, and to yield yourself to all subjection. Be fiercely against yourself, and suffer no swelling of pride to dwell in you. But show yourself so humble and so very small, that all may be able to walk over you, and to tread you down as the mire of the streets (Isa. 51:23).

What have you, O vain man, to complain of? What can you answer, foul sinner, to them that upbraid you, you who have so often offended God, and so many times deserved Hell? But My eye spared you, because your soul was precious in My sight; that you might know My love, and ever be thankful for My benefits. Also that you might continually give yourself to true subjection and humility, and endure patiently the contempt which belongs to you.

Chapter 14

THE SECRET JUDGMENTS OF GOD

THOU THUNDEREST FORTH Thy judgments over me, O Lord. Thou shakest all my bones with fear and trembling, and my soul is very sore afraid. I stand astonished; and I consider that "the heavens are not clean in his sight" (Job 15:15). If in angels Thou didst find wickedness (Job 4:18), and didst not spare even them, what shall become of me? Stars fell from Heaven (Rev. 8:10), and what can I presume who am dust? They whose works seem commendable have fallen into the depths, and those who did eat the bread of angels (Ps. 78:25), I have seen delighting themselves with the husks of swine (Luke 15:16).

No sanctity is there therefore, if Thou, O Lord, withdraw Thine hand. No wisdom availeth, if Thou cease to guide. No courage helpeth, if Thou leave off to preserve. No chastity is secure, if Thou do not protect it. No custody of our own availeth, if Thy sacred watchfulness be not present. For, left to ourselves, we sink and perish; but being visited of Thee, we are raised up and live. Unstable truly are we, but through Thee we are strengthened; we wax lukewarm, but by Thee we are inflamed.

Oh, how humbly and meanly ought I to think of myself! How ought I to esteem it as nothing, if I should seem to have aught of good! With what profound humility ought I to submit myself to Thy unfathomable judgments, O Lord; where I find myself to be nothing else than nothing, and still nothing! O weight unmeasurable! O sea that cannot be passed over, where I discover nothing of myself save only and wholly nothing!

Where then is the lurking place of glory? Where the confidence conceived of virtue? Swallowed up is all vaingloring in the deep of Thy judgments over me. What is all flesh in Thy sight? Shall the clay glory against him that formed it (Isa. 45:9; Rom. 9:20)? How can he be lifted up with vain words whose heart is truly subject to God (Isa. 29:16)? Not all the world shall lift up him whom the truth has subjected to itself. Neither shall he, who has firmly settled his whole hope in God, be moved with the tongues of any who praise him. For even they themselves who speak, behold, they all are nothing, for they will pass away with the sound of their words; but "the truth of the Lord endureth forever" (Ps. 117:2).

Chapter 15

HIS WILL IN EVERYTHING

My son, say thus in everything: "Lord, if this be pleasing unto Thee, so let it be (James 4:15). Lord, if it be to Thy honor, in Thy name let this be done. Lord, if Thou seest it expedient for me, and approvest it to be useful, then grant unto me that I may use this to Thine honor. But if Thou knowest it will be hurtful unto me, and no profit to the health of my soul, take away any such desire from me.

For not every desire proceeds from the Holy Spirit, even though it seem right and good. It is difficult to judge truly whether a good spirit or the contrary drive you to desire this or that; or whether by your own spirit you be moved thereto. Many have been deceived in the end, who at the first seemed to be led on by a good spirit.

Therefore whatever occurs to the mind as desirable must always be desired and prayed for in the fear of God and with humility of heart. You must commit the whole matter to Me with special resignation of yourself, and say: O Lord, Thou knowest what is the better way, let this or that be done, as Thou shalt please. Give what Thou wilt, and how much Thou wilt, and when Thou wilt. Deal with me as Thou knowest, and as best pleaseth Thee, and is most for Thy honor. Set me where Thou wilt, and deal with me in all things just as Thou wilt. I am in Thy hand: turn me round, and turn me back again, even as a wheel. Behold, I am Thy servant, prepared for all things; for I desire not to live unto myself, but unto Thee; and oh, that I could do it worthily and perfectly!

A prayer that the will of God may be fulfilled.

O most merciful Jesus, grant to me Thy grace, that it may be with me, and labor with me, and persevere with me even to the end.

Grant me always to desire and to will that which is to Thee most acceptable. Let Thy will be mine, and let my will ever follow Thine, and agree perfectly with it. Let my will be one with Thine, and let me not be able to will or not to will anything else, but what Thou willest or willest not.

Grant that I may die to all things that are in the world, and for Thy sake love to be condemned and not known in this generation. Grant to me above all things that can be desired, to rest in Thee, and in Thee to have my heart at peace. Thou art the true peace of the heart; Thou its only rest; out of Thee all things are hard and restless. In this peace, in this selfsame thing, that is, in Thee, the chiefest eternal good, I will sleep and rest (Ps. 4:8). Amen.

Chapter 16

TRUE COMFORT FOUND IN GOD ALONE

WHATEVER I DESIRE or can imagine for my comfort, I look for it hereafter. For if I might alone have all the comforts of the world, and were able to enjoy all the delights thereof (Matt. 16:26), it is certain that they could not long endure.

You cannot be fully comforted (Ps. 77:1, 2), nor have perfect refreshment, except in God, the Comforter of the poor, and Patron of the humble. Wait a little while, O my soul, wait for the divine promise, and you shall have abundance of all good things in Heaven.

If you desire inordinately the things that are present, you shall lose those which are heavenly and eternal. Let temporal things be used, but things eternal desired.

You cannot be satisfied with any temporal good, because you were not created to enjoy these alone.

Although you should possess all created good, yet you could not be happy therewith nor blessed; but in God, who created all things, consists your whole blessedness. Not such as is seen and commended by the foolish lovers of the world, but such as the good and faithful servants of Christ wait for, and of which the spiritual and pure in heart, whose conversation is in Heaven (Phil. 3:20), sometimes have a foretaste.

All human comfort is vain and brief. Blessed and true is the comfort which is received inwardly from the truth.

A devout man bears everywhere with him his own Comforter Jesus, and says unto Him: "Be Thou present with me, O Lord Jesus, in every time and place. Let this be my consolation, to be cheerfully willing to do without all human comfort. And if Thy consolation be wanting, let Thy will, and just trial of me be unto me as the greatest comfort." "He will not always chide: neither will he keep his anger forever" (Ps. 103:9).

Chapter 17

ALL ANXIETIES CAST ON GOD

MY SON, suffer Me to do with you what I please; I know what is expedient for you. You think as man; you judge in many things as human feelings persuade you.

O Lord, what Thou sayest is true. Greater is Thy anxiety for me (Matt. 6:30; John 6:20) than all the care that I can take for myself. For he stands very unsteadily who casts not all his anxiety upon Thee (I Peter 5:7).

O Lord, if only my will may remain right and firm toward Thee, do with me whatever it shall please Thee. For it cannot be anything but good, whatever Thou shalt do with me. If Thou willest me to be in darkness, be Thou blessed; and if Thou willest me to be in light, be Thou again blessed. If Thou vouchsafe to comfort me, be Thou blessed; and if Thou willest me to be afflicted, be Thou ever equally blessed.

My son, such as this ought to be your state, if you desire to walk with Me. You ought to be as ready to suffer as to rejoice. You ought as cheerfuly to be destitute and poor, as full and rich.

O Lord, cheerfully will I suffer for Thy sake (Job 2:10), whatever Thou shalt will to come upon me. From Thy hand I am willing to receive indifferently good and evil, sweet and bitter, joy and sorrow, and for all that befalleth me to give Thee thanks.

Keep me safe from all sin, and I shall fear neither death (Ps. 23:4) nor Hell. Cast me not from Thee forever, nor blot me out of the Book of Life (Rev. 3:5), and whatever tribulation may come upon me shall not hurt me.

Chapter 18

TEMPORAL MISERIES BORNE
PATIENTLY

My SON, I came down from Heaven (John 3:13) for your salvation. I took upon Me your miseries (Isa. 53:4), not necessity but love drawing Me, that you might learn patience, and bear temporal miseries without grudging. For from the hour of My birth, even until My death on the cross, I was not without grief. I suffered want of things temporal; I often heard complaints against Me; I endured calmly disgraces and revilings; for benefits I received ingratitude; for miracles, blasphemies; for teaching, reproofs.

O Lord, for that Thou wast patient in Thy lifetime, herein especially fulfilling the commandment of Thy Father (John 5:30), worthy it is that I, a most miserable sinner, according to Thy will should bear myself patiently, and for my welfare endure the burden of this corruptible life as long as Thou shalt will. For although this present life is burdensome, yet notwithstanding it is now by Thy grace made gainful; and by Thy example and the footsteps of Thy saints, brighter and more bearable to the weak. There is, moreover, much more consolation than formerly under the old Law, when the gate of Heaven remained shut. And the way also to Heaven seemed darker, when so few sought the kingdom of Heaven (Matt. 7:14). Moreover, also they who then were just and meet to be saved could not enter into the heavenly kingdom before Thy passion and Thy holy death.

How great thanks am I bound to render unto Thee, that Thou hast vouchsafed to show unto Me and to all faithful people the good and the right way to Thine eternal kingdom! For Thy life is our way, and by holy patience we walk toward Thee who art our Crown. If Thou hadst not gone before us and taught us, who would care to follow? Alas, how many would remain behind and afar off, if they did not gaze upon Thy glorious example! Behold, even yet we are lukewarm, though we have heard of so many of Thy miracles and teachings. What would become of us if we had not so great light (Heb. 12:46) whereby to follow Thee!

Chapter 19

ENDURANCE OF INJURIES. WHO IS PATIENT?

WHAT IS IT YOU SAY, My son? Cease to complain, when you consider My passion, and the sufferings of others. You "have not yet resisted unto blood" (Heb. 12:4). It is but little which you suffer in comparison with those who suffered so many things, who were so strongly tempted, so heavily afflicted, in so many ways tried and exercised (Heb. 11:37). You ought therefore to call to mind the severer sufferings of others, that you may the easier bear your own small troubles. And if they seem not very small, then beware lest your impatience be the cause. However, whether they be small or great, endeavor patiently to endure them all. The better you prepare yourself to suffer, the wiser you are, and the greater reward shall you receive. You shall also more easily endure, if both in mind and by habit you have diligently prepared to meet suffering.

Do not say: "I cannot endure to suffer these things at the hands of this man, nor ought I to endure things of this sort. He has done me grievous harm, and reproaches me with things which I never thought of. But of another I will willingly suffer, and will look upon them as things which I ought to suffer."

Foolish is such a thought. It considers not the virtue of patience, nor by whom it will be crowned; but rather weighs the persons and the injuries offered to oneself. He is not truly patient, who wills to suffer only so much as he thinks good, and from whom he pleases. But the truly patient man minds not by whom he is exercised, whether by his superior, by one of his equals, or by an inferior; whether by a good and holy man, or by one that is perverse and unworthy. But indifferently from every creature, how much or how often anything adverse befall him, he takes all thankfully as from the hand of God, and esteems it a great gain. For with God it is impossible that anything, however small, if only it be suffered for God's sake, should pass without its reward.

Be therefore prepared for the fight, if you will have the victory. Without a combat you cannot receive the crown of patience (II Tim. 2:3-5). If you will not to suffer, you refuse to be crowned. But if you desire to be crowned, strive manfully, endure patiently. Without labor there is no arriving at rest, nor without fighting can the victory be reached.

O Lord, let that become possible to me by grace, which by nature seems to me impossible! Thou knowest that I am able to suffer but little, and that I am quickly cast down, when a slight adversity arises. For Thy name's sake, let every exercise of tribulation be made lovable and desirable to me; for to suffer and to be disquieted for Thy sake is very wholesome for my soul.

Chapter 20

ACKNOWLEDGE INFIRMITY AND THE MISERIES OF LIFE

I ACKNOWLEDGED my sin unto thee" (Ps. 32:5); I will confess my weakness unto Thee, O Lord. Oftentimes it is a small matter that casts down and makes me sad. I resolve that I will act with courage, but when even a small temptation comes, I am at once in a great strait. It is sometimes a trifle, from which a heavy temptation arises. And while I am thinking myself tolerably safe, and when I feel it not, I sometimes find myself almost entirely overcome by a slight breath.

Behold therefore, O Lord, my low estate (Ps. 25: 18), and my frailty which is known unto Thee! Have mercy on me, and "deliver me out of the mire, and let me not sink" (Ps. 69:14), that I remain not utterly cast down forever. This is that which oftentimes strikes me down, and confounds me in Thy sight, that I am so subject to fall, and weak in resisting my passions. And although I do not altogether consent, yet their continued assaulting is troublesome and grievous unto me; and it is exceedingly weary to live thus daily in conflict. From hence my weakness becomes known unto me, in that hateful phantoms do always much more easily rush in than depart.

Most mighty God of Israel, Thou zealous Lover of faithful souls! Oh, that Thou wouldst consider the labor and sorrow of Thy servant, and stand by him in all things, whatever he reaches forward to do! Strengthen me with heavenly courage, lest the old man, the miserable flesh, not as yet fully subject to the Spirit, prevail and get the upper hand; against which it will be needful for me to fight, so long as I breathe in this most miserable life.

Alas, what kind of life is this, where tribulation and miseries are never wanting; where all is full of snares and enemies! For when one tribulation or temptation retreats, another comes. Yea, and while the first conflict is still on, many others come unexpected one after another.

And how can a life be loved that has so many embitterments, and is subject to so many calamities and miseries? How too can it be called life, that begets so many deaths and plagues? And yet it is loved, and many seek to delight themselves therein. The world is oftentimes blamed for being deceitful and vain, and yet it is not easily abandoned, because the desires of the flesh are so strong. But some things draw us to love the world, others to condemn it. "The lust of the flesh, and the lust of the eyes, and the pride of life" (I John 2:16) draw us to the love of the world. But the pains and miseries that follow them bring a hatred of the world and a weariness thereof. But alas, vicious pleasure overcomes the mind that is addicted to the world; and to be under thorns (Job 30:7) it esteems a delight, because it has neither seen nor tasted the sweetness of God, and the inward pleasantness of virtue.

But they who perfectly condemn the world, and study to live to God under holy discipline, these are not ignorant of the divine sweetness promised to those who truly renounce the world. They also see very clearly how grievously the world errs, and is in many ways deceived.

Chapter 21

REST IN GOD ABOVE ALL THINGS

ABOVE ALL THINGS, and in all things, O my soul, rest in the Lord alway, for He is the everlasting rest of the saints.

Grant me, O loving Jesus, to rest in Thee above every creature (Rom. 8:19-22); above all health and beauty, above all glory and honor, above all power and dignity, above all knowledge and subtility, above all riches and arts, above all joy and gladness, above all fame and praise, above all sweetness and comfort, above all hope and promise, above all desert and desire. Above all gifts and favors that Thou canst give and pour upon us, above all mirth and exultation that the mind can receive and feel; finally, all the host of Heaven, above all finally, above angels and archangels, and above all the host of Heaven, above all things visible and invisible, and above all that is not Thee, my God.

Because Thou, O Lord my God, art above all things the best; Thou alone art most high, Thou alone most powerful, Thou alone most sufficient and most full, Thou alone most sweet and most full of consolation. Thou alone art most lovely and loving, Thou alone most noble and glorious above all things; in whom all good things together both perfectly are, and ever have been, and shall be. And therefore it is too small, and unsatisfying, whatever Thou bestowest on me besides Thyself, or revealest unto me of Thyself, or promisest, whilst Thou art not seen, nor fully obtained. For surely my heart cannot truly rest, nor be entirely contented, unless it rest in Thee, and surmount all gifts and every creature..

O Thou most beloved Bridegroom of my soul, Jesus Christ, Thou most pure Lover, Thou Lord of all creation, who will give me the wings of true liberty, that I might flee away and rest in Thee (Ps. 55:6)! Oh, when shall it be fully granted me, to consider in quietness of mind and see how sweet Thou art, O Lord my God! When shall I fully gather up myself into Thee, that by reason of my love to Thee I may not feel myself, but Thee alone, above all thought and measure, in a manner not all men know. But now I oftentimes groan, and bear my unhappiness with grief. Because many evils occur in this vale of miseries, which do often trouble, sadden, and overcloud me; often hinder and distract me, allure and entangle me, so that I can have no free access unto Thee, nor enjoy the sweet welcomings which are ever ready with the blessed spirits.

Let my sighs move Thee and my manifold desolation here on earth, O Jesus, Thou brightness of the eternal glory (Heb. 1:3), Thou comfort of the pilgrim soul. With Thee is my tongue without voice, and my very silence speaks to Thee. How long does my Lord delay to come? Let Him come to me His poor despised servant, and make me glad. Let Him put forth His hand, and deliver me in my misery from all anguish. Come, O come; for without Thee no day or hour shall be glad; for Thou art my gladness, and without Thee my table is empty. In misery am I, and in a manner imprisoned and loaded with fetters, until Thou refresh me with the light of Thy presence, and grant me liberty, and show a friendly countenance toward me. Let others seek what else they please instead of Thee; but for me, nothing else meanwhile pleases nor shall please me, but Thou only, my God, my hope, my everlasting salvation. I will not hold my peace, nor cease to pray, until Thy grace return again, and Thou speak inwardly to me.

Behold, here I am! Behold, I come unto thee, because thou hast called upon Me! Thy tears and the desire of thy soul, thy humiliation and thy contrition of heart, have inclined and brought Me unto thee.

And I said, Lord, I have called Thee, and have desired to enjoy Thee, being ready to spurn all things for Thy sake. For Thou didst first stir me up that I might seek Thee. Blessed be Thou therefore, O Lord, that hast shown this goodness to Thy servant, according to the multitude of Thy mercies. What hath Thy servant more to say before Thee, but that he greatly humble himself in Thy sight, ever mindful of his own iniquity and vileness. For there is none like unto Thee (Ps. 86:8) in all the wonderful things of Heaven and earth. Thy works are very good, Thy judgments true, and by Thy providence the universe is ruled. Praise therefore and glory be unto Thee, O wisdom of the Father; let my mouth, my soul, and all created things together praise and bless Thee.

Chapter 22

GOD'S MANIFOLD BENEFITS

OPEN, O LORD, my heart in Thy law, and teach me to walk in Thy commandments (Ps. 119). Grant me to understand Thy will, and with great reverence and diligent consideration to remember Thy benefits, in general as well as in particular, that henceforth I may be able worthily to give Thee thanks. But I know, and confess, that I am not able, even in the least point, to give Thee due thanks and praises. I am less than any of the benefits bestowed upon me (Gen. 32:10); and when I consider Thy excellency, my spirit faints before its greatness.

All that we have in soul and in body, and whatever we possess outwardly or inwardly, by nature or beyond nature, are Thy benefits, and proclaim Thee bountiful, merciful, and good, from whom we have received all good things.

Although one have received more, another less, all notwithstanding are Thine, and without Thee even the least blessing cannot be had.

He who has received greater cannot glory in his own

desert, nor extol himself above others, nor insult the lesser. For he is the greatest and the best, who ascribes least to himself, and who in rendering thanks is the humblest and the most devout. And he who esteems himself viler than all men, and judges himself most unworthy, is fittest to receive the greater blessings.

But he who has received fewer blessings ought not to be discouraged, nor to take it grievously, nor envy him that is richer. But rather he should turn his mind to Thee, and exceedingly praise Thy goodness, for that Thou bestowest Thy gifts so bountifully, so freely, and so willingly, without respect of persons.

All things proceed from Thee, and therefore in all Thou art to be praised.

Thou knowest what is fit to be given to every one; and why this man should have less, and that more, this is not for us to judge, but for Thee with whom every man's deserts are exactly marked.

Wherefore, O Lord God, I even esteem it a great mercy, not to have much of that which outwardly and in the opinion of men seems worthy of glory and applause. For so it comes, that he who considers the poverty and unworthiness of his own person, is so far from conceiving grief or sadness, or from being cast down, that he takes great comfort and is glad; because Thou, O God, hast chosen the poor and humble and the despised of this world for Thyself (I Cor. 1:27, 28), for Thy familiar friends and household. Witnesses are Thy apostles, and yet they lived in the world without complaint (I Thess. 2:10), so humble and simple, without all malice and deceit, that they even rejoiced to suffer reproaches for Thy name (Acts 5: 41); and what the world abhors they embraced with great affection.

Nothing therefore ought so to rejoice him that loves Thee and knows Thy benefits, as Thy will toward him, and the good pleasure of Thy eternal appointment. And therewith he ought to be so contented and comforted, that he would as willingly be the least, as another would wish to be the greatest. And he would be as peacable and contented in the last place as in the first; as willing to be a despised castaway, of no name or great report, as to be preferred in honor before others, and to be greater in the world than they. For Thy will and the love of Thy honor ought to surpass all things, and to comfort him more, and please him better, than all the benefits which he either has received or can receive.

Chapter 23

INWARD PEACE

M Y SON, now will I teach you the way of peace and true liberty.

Do, O Lord, as Thou sayest, for this is well-pleasing to me to hear.

Be desirous, My son, to do the will of another rather than your own (Matt. 26:39; John 5:30; 6:38). Choose always to have less rather than more (I Cor.

10:24). Seek always the lower place, and to be inferior to every one (Luke 14:10). Wish always, and pray, that the will of God be wholly done in you (Matt. 6:10). Such a man enters within the borders of peace and rest.

O Lord, this short discourse contains within itself much perfection (Matt. 5:48). It is little to be spoken, but full of meaning, and abundant in fruit. For if it could faithfully be kept by me, trouble ought not so easily to arise in me. For as often as I feel myself unquiet and weighed down, I find that I have gone back from this doctrine. But Thou who canst do all things, and ever lovest the profiting of my soul, add unto me greater grace, that I may be able to fulfill Thy words.

A prayer against evil thoughts.

"O God, be not far from me: O my God, make haste for my help" (Ps. 71:12). For there have risen up against me many thoughts, and great fears, afflicting my soul. How shall I pass through unhurt? How shall I break them to pieces?

He saith: "I will go before thee, and make the crooked places straight . . . I will give thee the treasures of darkness, and hidden riches of secret places" (Isa. 45:2, 3).

Do, O Lord, as Thou sayest, and let all evil thoughts fly from before Thy face. This is my hope, my only consolation, to flee unto Thee from my inmost heart, and to wait patiently for Thy consolation.

A prayer for mental illumination.

O Lord Jesus, enlighten me with the clear shining of an inward light, and remove all darkness from the

141

habitation of my heart. Repress my many wandering thoughts, and break in pieces those temptations which violently assault me. Fight strongly for me, and vanquish the evil beasts, the alluring desires of the flesh. So there may be peace in Thy walls (Ps. 122:7), and that Thine abundant praise may resound in Thy holy court, that is, in a pure conscience. Command the winds and tempests; say unto the sea, Be still; say to the north wind, Blow not; and there shall be a great calm.

"Send out thy light and thy truth" (Ps. 43:3), that they may shine upon the earth; for I am earth without form and void until Thou enlighten me. Pour forth Thy grace from above, shower upon my heart the dew of Heaven, supply fresh streams of devotion to water the face of the earth, that it may bring forth fruit good and excellent. Lift up my mind which is pressed down by a load of sins, and draw up my whole desire to things heavenly; that having tasted the sweetness of supernal happiness, it may be irksome to me to think of earthly things.

Pluck me away, and deliver me from all unenduring comfort of creatures; for no created thing can give full rest and comfort to my desires. Join me to Thyself with an inseparable band of love; for Thou even alone dost satisfy him who loves Thee; and without Thee all things are vain and frivolous.

Chapter 24

AVOID CURIOUS INQUIRIES

My son, be not curious, nor trouble yourself with idle anxieties (I Tim. 5:13). What is this or that to thee? "Follow thou me" (John 21:22). For what is it to you, whether that man be such or such, or whether this man do or speak this or that? You shall not need to answer for others, but shall give account for yourself. Why therefore entangle yourself? Behold, I know all men, and see all things that are done under the sun. Also I understand how it is with every one, what he thinks, what he wills, and to what end his intention aims. Unto Me therefore all things are to be committed; but keep yourself in perfect peace, and let go the unquiet, to be as unquiet as he will. Whatever he shall have done or said shall come upon him, for he cannot deceive Me.

Be not careful for the shadow of a great name, nor for the familiar friendship of many, nor for the private affection of men. For these things bring distractions, and great darkness in the heart. Willingly would I speak My word, and reveal My hidden things, if you would diligently observe My coming, and open to Me the door of your heart. Be circumspect and watchful in prayer, and in all things humble yourself.

Chapter 25

PEACE OF HEART AND TRUE SPIRITUAL PROGRESS

M Y SON, I have spoken: "Peace I leave with you, my peace I give unto you: not as the world giveth, give I unto you" (John 14:27). Peace is what all desire, but all do not care for the things that make for true peace. My peace is with the humble and gentle of heart; in much patience shall your peace be. If you will hear Me and follow My voice, you shall enjoy much peace.

What then shall I do?

In every matter look to yourself, what you do and what you say; and direct your whole intention to this, that you may please Me alone, and neither desire nor seek anything besides Me. But of the words or deeds of others judge nothing rashly; neither entangle yourself with things not committed to you; and you will be little or seldom disturbed. But never to feel any disturbance at all, nor to suffer any trouble of heart or body, belongs not to the present time, but to the state of eternal rest.

Think not therefore that you have found true peace, if you feel no heaviness; nor that then all is well, if you are vexed with no adversary; nor that this is to be perfect, if all things happen according to your desire. Neither esteem yourself at all highly nor account yourself to be specially beloved, if you be in a state of great devotion and sweetness. For it is not by these things that a true lover of virtue is known, nor in these things consists the progress and perfection of a man.

Wherein then, O Lord?

In giving yourself over with all your heart to the divine will, not seeking your own things, either great or small, either in time or in eternity. So shall you keep an even countenance, in thanksgiving, amid prosperity and adversity, weighing all things with an equal balance. Be so brave, and so longsuffering in hope, that when inward comfort is withdrawn, you may prepare your heart to suffer even greater things. Do not justify yourself, as though you ought not to suffer these afflictions or any so great, but justify Me in whatever I appoint, and praise My holy name. Then you are walking in the true and right way of peace, and shall have undoubted hope to see My face again with great delight. For if you attain to the full contempt of yourself, know that you shall then enjoy abundance of peace, as great as your state of sojourning is able to possess.

Chapter 26

A FREE MIND WON BY HUMBLE PRAYER

O LORD, this is the business of a perfect man, never to relax his mind from attentive thought of heavenly things, and amid many cares to pass by, as it were, without care. Not as one destitute of all feeling, but by a certain privilege of a free mind, cleaving to no creature with inordinate affection.

I beseech Thee, most gracious God, preserve me from the cares of this life, that I may not be too entangled therein; from the many necessities of the body, that I may not be ensnared by pleasure; from whatever is an obstacle to the soul, that I may not be broken with troubles and overthrown. I do not say, preserve me from those things which worldly vanity with its whole affection compasses, but from those miseries, which as punishments by the common curse of mortality (Gen. 3:17; Rom. 7:23, 24) weigh down and hinder the soul of Thy servant, that it cannot enter into the freedom of the Spirit, as often as it would.

O my God, Thou sweetness ineffable, turn for me into bitterness all carnal comfort, which draws me away from the love of things eternal, and in evil manner allures me to itself by the view of some present delightsome good. O my God, let me not be overcome by flesh and blood (Rom. 12:21); let not the world and the brief glory thereof deceive me; let not the Devil and his cunning make me fall. Give me strength to resist, patience to endure, and constancy to persevere. Give me instead of all the comforts of the world, the sweetest unction of Thy Spirit, and in place of carnal love pour in the love of Thy name.

Behold, meat, drink, raiment, and all the other necessities for the maintenance of the body are burdensome to a fervent spirit. Grant me to use such refreshments moderately, and not to be entangled with an overly great desire of them. To cast away all things is not lawful, because nature is to be sustained; but to require superfluities, and those things that give the more delight, the holy Law forbids. For then the flesh would wax wanton against the Spirit. Herein, I beseech Thee, let Thy hand govern me and teach me, that there may be no excess.

Chapter 27

PRIVATE LOVE HINDERS THE CHIEFEST GOOD

MY SON, you ought to give all for all, and to be nothing of yourself. Know that love of yourself hurts more than anything in the world. According to the love and affection which you bear toward anything, so it more or less cleaves to you. If your love is pure (Matt. 6:22), simple, and well-ordered, you shall be free from the bondage of things.

Do not covet that which it is not lawful to have. Do not have that which may entangle and deprive you of inward liberty. It is strange that you commit not yourself wholly to Me from the bottom of your heart, with all things you can have or desire. Why are you consumed with vain grief (Exod. 18:18; Micah 4:9)? Why weary yourself with superfluous cares? Be resigned to My good pleasure, and you shall suffer no loss.

If you seek this or that, and would be in another place, to enjoy your own profit and pleasure, you shall never be at rest, nor free from anxiety. For in every instance something will be found wanting, and in every place there will be someone to cross you.

Man's welfare then lies not in obtaining or multiplying any external thing, but rather in despising it, and utterly rooting it out from the heart. And this you must understand not only of income of money and riches, but of seeking after honor also, and the desire of vain praise, which pass away with this world.

The place gives little defense if the spirit of fervor is lacking, neither shall that peace long continue which is sought abroad (Isa. 41:13). If the state of your heart is destitute of a true foundation, that is, unless you stand steadfast in Me, you may change but not better yourself. For when occasion arises and is laid hold of, you shall find what you fled from, and more also.

A prayer for a clean heart and heavenly wisdom.

Confirm me, O God, by the grace of Thy Holy Spirit (Ps. 51:12). Grant me might to be strengthened in the inner man (Eph. 3:16), and to empty my heart of all useless anxiety and distress (Matt. 6:34); not to be drawn away with desires of anything whatever, whether mean or precious, but to look on all things as passing away, and on myself as about to pass away with them. For nothing is abiding under the sun, where "all is vanity and vexation of spirit" (Eccles. 1:14; 2:17, 26). Oh, how wise is he who so considers them!

Grant me, O Lord, heavenly wisdom, that I may learn above all things to seek and to find Thee, above all things to relish and to love Thee, and to think of all other things as being, what indeed they are, at the disposal of Thy wisdom. Help me to avoid him who flatters me, and to endure patiently him who opposes me. Because this is great wisdom, not to be moved with every kind of words (Eph. 4:14), nor to give ear to flattery; for so we shall go on securely in the way which we have begun.

Chapter 28

THE TONGUES OF SLANDERERS

M Y SON, take it not grievously if some think ill of
you (I Cor. 4:13), and speak that which you
would not willingly hear. You ought to judge the
worst of yourself, and to think no man weaker than
yourself.

If you walk inwardly, you will not weigh passing
words. It is prudent to keep silence in an evil time
(Amos 5:13), and to turn to Me, and not to be
troubled by the judgment of men.

Let not your peace be in the tongues of men; for
whether they interpret well or ill you are not therefore another man.

Where are true peace and glory? Are they not in
Me (John 16:33)? And he who neither covets to
please men, nor fears to displease them, shall enjoy
much peace. From inordinate love and vain fear arise
all disquietness of heart and distraction of the
thoughts.

Chapter 29

CALL UPON GOD WHEN
TRIBULATION COMES

BLESSED BE THY NAME, O Lord, forever (Ps. 113:2) who hast willed that this temptation and tribulation should come upon me. I cannot escape it, but must needs flee to Thee, that Thou mayest help me, and turn it to my good.

Lord, I am now in tribulation, and my heart is ill at ease, for I am much troubled with the present suffering. And now, O beloved Father, what shall I say? I am caught amid straits; "Save me from this hour: but for this cause came I unto this hour" (John 12:27), that Thou mayest be glorified, when I shall have been greatly humbled, and by Thee delivered. "Be pleased, O Lord, to deliver me" (Ps. 40:13), for, poor wretch that I am, what can I do, and where shall I go without Thee? Grant me patience, O Lord, even now in this moment. Help me, my God, and then I will not fear how grievously I am afflicted.

And now amid these things what shall I say? Lord, "thy will be done" (Matt. 6:10); I have deserved to be afflicted and weighed down. Assuredly I ought to bear it; and oh, that I may bear it with patience until the tempest pass over! Howbeit Thy Almighty hand hath power to take even this temptation from me, and to assuage the violence thereof, that I sink not under it; as oftentimes heretofore Thou hast dealt with me, O my God, my Mercy! And the more difficult it is to me, so much the easier to Thee is this change "of the right hand of the Most High" (Ps. 77:10).

Chapter 30

SEEK DIVINE AID, AND RECOVER GRACE

M Y SON, I am the Lord, "a stronghold in the day of trouble" (Nahum 1:7). "Come unto me," whenever it shall not be well with you (Matt. 11:28).

This most of all hinders heavenly consolation, that you are slow in turning to prayer. For before you earnestly ask of Me, you seek other comforts, and refresh yourself in outward things. And so it comes to pass that all profits you little, until you remember that it is I who bring that hope in Me; and that outside of Me there is neither powerful help, nor profitable counsel, nor lasting remedy.

But, having now recovered breath after the tempest, gather strength again in the light of My tender mercies. For I am at hand, saith the Lord, to repair all, not only entirely, but also abundantly and with increase. Is there anything too hard for Me? Or shall

I be like one that says and does not (Matt. 23:3)? Where is your faith? Stand firmly and with perseverance; be longsuffering, and a man of courage; comfort will come in due time. Wait for Me, yea, wait; I will come and heal you (Matt. 8:7).

It is a temptation that vexes you, and a vain fear that affrights you. What else does anxiety about future accidents bring but sorrow upon sorrow? "Sufficient unto the day is the evil thereof" (Matt. 6:34). It is a vain thing and unprofitable, to be either disturbed or pleased about future things, which perhaps will never come to pass. But it belongs to man's nature to be deluded with such imaginations; and it is a sign of a weak mind to be so easily drawn away at the suggestions of the Enemy. For he cares not whether it is by things true or false that he delude and deceive; nor whether he overthrow you with the love of present or the fear of future things. "Let not your heart be troubled, neither let it be afraid" (John 14:27). Trust in Me, and have confidence in My mercy (Ps. 91:2). When you think yourself far from Me, oftentimes I am the nearest. When you count almost all to be lost, then oftentimes the greater gain of reward is close at hand. All is not lost, when anything falls out contrary. You ought not to judge according to present feeling; nor to take any heaviness, or give yourself over to it, from wherever it comes, as though all hope of rising therefrom were taken away. Think not yourself wholly left, although for a time I have sent some tribulation, or even have withdrawn desired comfort; for this is the passage to the kingdom of Heaven.

And without doubt, it is more expedient for you and the rest of My servants, to be exercised with adversities, than that you should have all things according to your desires. I know the secret thoughts, and that it is very expedient for your welfare that you be left sometimes without taste of spiritual sweetness, lest you should be puffed up with your prosperous state, and desire to please yourself in that which you are not. That which I have given, I can take away; and I can restore it again when I please. When I give it, it is Mine; when I withdraw it, I have not taken anything that is yours; for Mine is "every good gift and every perfect gift" (James 1:17). If I send affliction, or any cross whatever, grieve not, nor let your heart fail you; I can quickly comfort you and turn all your burden into joy. But I am righteous, and greatly to be praised when I deal thus with you. If you are wise, and consider what the truth is, you never ought to be cast down and saddened because of adversities, but rather to rejoice and give thanks. Yea, you will account this your special joy, that I afflict you with sorrow, and do not spare you. "As the Father hath loved me, so have I loved you" (John 15:9), I said to My beloved disciples. I sent them out not to temporal joys, but to great conflicts; not to honors, but to contempts; not to idleness, but to labors; not to rest, but to bring forth much "fruit with patience" (Luke 8:15). Remember these words, My son!

Chapter 31

DISREGARD OF CREATURE

O LORD, I stand in need of great grace, if I ought to reach that place where no man or any creature shall be a hindrance to me.

For as long as anything holds me back, I cannot freely flee to Thee. He was longing to flee freely who said: "Oh that I had wings like a dove! For then would I fly away, and be at rest" (Ps. 55:6). What is more at rest than the single eye (Matt. 6:22)? And what is more free than he who desires nothing upon earth? A man ought therefore to mount over every creature, and perfectly to forsake himself and stand spellbound, and see that Thou, the Creator of all things, hast nothing among creatures like unto Thyself. Unless too a man be disentangled from all creatures, he cannot freely attend to divine things. For that is the reason why there are few contemplative men to be found, because few have the knowledge to withdraw themselves fully from things about to perish and from creatures.

To obtain this there is need of much grace, which may elevate the soul and carry it away above itself.

And unless a man be elevated in spirit, and freed from all creatures, and wholly united unto God, whatever he knows, and whatever he has, is of no great weight. For a long while he will be small and lie groveling below, who esteems anything great, but the One only infinite eternal Good. And whatever is not God, is nothing, and ought to be accounted as nothing.

There is great difference between the wisdom of an illuminated and devout man, and the knowledge of a learned and studious man. Far nobler is that learning which flows from above, from the divine outpouring, than that which is painfully acquired by the wit of man.

Many are found who desire contemplation, but they have no mind to practice the things that are required thereunto. It is a great hindrance that men rest in signs and sensible things, and care little about the perfect mortification of themselves.

I know not what it is, or by what spirit we are led, or what we pretend, we that seem to be called spiritual, that we take so much pains, and are so full of anxiety about transitory and mean things, while we seldom, and hardly at all with full recollection of mind, think of our own inward concerns. Alas, presently after a slight recollection we burst forth abroad, and weigh not our works with strict examination. We mind not where our affections lie, nor bewail the impurity that is in all our actions. For "all flesh had corrupted his way," and therefore did the great deluge follow (Gen. 6:12; 7:21). Since then our inward affection is much corrupted; our actions from thence proceeding, which are the proof of the lack of inward strength, must needs be corrupted also. From a pure heart proceeds the fruit of a good life (Matt. 7:16).

We ask how much a man has done; but from what degree of virtue he acts is not so carefully weighed. We inquire whether he has been courageous, rich, handsome, skillful, a good writer, a good singer, or a good laborer. But how poor he is in spirit, how patient and meek, how devout and spiritual, of this most men hold their peace! Nature respects the outward things of a man, grace turns itself to the inward. The one is often disappointed; the other hopes in God, and so is not deceived.

Chapter 32

SELF-DENIAL

My son, you cannot possess perfect liberty unless you wholly renounce yourself (Matt. 16:24; 19:21).

Bound in fetters are all they who seek their own interest, and are lovers of themselves—covetous, inquisitive, wandering in a circle, seeking ever soft and delicate things, not the things of Jesus Christ, but oftentimes devising and framing that which will not stand. For it shall perish altogether, whatever is not born of God.

Keep this short and perfect word: Let go all and you shall find all; leave desire and you shall find rest. Weigh this thoroughly in your mind, and when you have fulfilled it you shall understand all things.

O Lord, this is not the work of one day, nor children's sport. In this short word is included all the perfection of religious persons.

My son, you ought not to turn away, nor be cast down, when you hear the way of the perfect; but should rather be stirred up to higher things, and at least in desire to sigh after them.

I would it were so with you, and you were no longer a lover of yourself, but that you stand merely at My beck, and at his whom I have appointed over you. Then you would exceedingly please Me, and all your life would pass away in joy and peace. You have yet many things to part with, which unless you wholly resign to Me, you shall not attain to that which you ask.

"I counsel thee to buy of me gold tried in the fire, that thou mayest be rich" (Rev. 3:18); that is, the heavenly wisdom, which treads under foot all that is mean and low. Put aside earthly wisdom, and all desire to please the world and yourself.

I said that you must buy mean things instead of things which, among men, are precious and exalted. For true heavenly wisdom seems very mean and small, and almost given up to forgetfulness, because she has no high thoughts of herself, nor seeks to be magnified upon earth. Many indeed praise her with their mouths, but in their lives they are far from her. Yet she is the "pearl of great price" (Matt. 13:46), which is hidden from many.

Chapter 33

INCONSTANCY OF HEART, AND
FINAL INTENTION

M Y SON, trust not to your present feeling; it shall
be quickly changed into another. As long as you
live, you are subject to mutability (Job 14:2), even
against your will. So that you are found one time
while merry, another while sad; one while quiet, another while troubled; now devout, then undevout;
now diligent, then listless; now grave, and then light.

But he who is wise and well-instructed in the Spirit
stands above these changeful things, not heeding what
he feels in himself or which way the wind of instability
blows; but the whole intention of his mind makes
progress to the due and desired end. For thus he will
be able to continue throughout one and the selfsame
and unshaken; in the midst of so many various issues
the single eye of his intention being directed unceasingly toward Me.

And the purer the eye of the intention is (Matt.
6:22), with so much the more constancy does a man
pass through divers storms.

But in many the eye of a pure intention waxes dim,
for their regard is quickly drawn aside to some pleas-
urable object which meets them. For it is rare to find

159

one who is wholly free from all blemish of self-seeking. So the Jews of old came to Bethany to Martha and Mary, not for Jesus' sake only, but that they might see Lazarus (John 12:9).

The eye of our intention therefore is to be purged, that it may be single and right (Matt. 6:22); and it is to be directed toward Me, beyond all the various objects which may come between.

Chapter 34

GOD IS SWEET TO THOSE WHO LOVE HIM

BEHOLD, MY GOD, and my all! What can I desire more, and what happier thing can I long for? O sweet and delicious Word! But to him only who loves the Word, not the world, nor the things that are in the world.

My God, and my all! To him who understands, enough has been said; and to repeat it often is delightful to him who loves.

When Thou art present, all things are delightful, but when Thou art absent, all things are loathsome. Thou makest a quiet heart, and great peace, and festal joy. Thou makest us to think well of all circumstances, and in all to praise Thee; neither can anything please long without Thee. But if it must needs be pleasant and of a good savor, Thy grace must be present, and it must be seasoned with the seasoning of Thy wisdom. What will not be of good savor unto him to whom Thou savorest well? And him to whom Thou savorest not, what shall have power to please?

But the wise men of the world, and they also who relish the things of the flesh, are found wanting in Thy wisdom (I Cor. 1:26; Rom. 8:5; I John 2:16); for in the world is found the utmost vanity, and in the flesh is found death. But they who follow Thee by the contempt of worldly things, and mortification of the flesh, are known to be truly wise; for they are brought over from vanity to truth, from the flesh to the spirit. To these God savors well; and what good is found in creatures, they wholly refer to the praise of their Maker. Different, however, yea, very different is the savor of the Creator and of the creature, of eternity and of time, of light uncreated and of light received.

O everlasting Light, surpassing all created luminaries, "cast forth thy lightning" (Ps. 144:6) from above, piercing all the most inward parts of my heart. Make clean, make glad, make bright, and make alive my spirit, with all the powers thereof, that I may cleave unto Thee in ecstasies of joy. When will that blessed and desired hour come, that Thou mayest satisfy me with Thy presence, and be unto me all in all! So long as this is not granted me I shall not have full joy.

Still, alas, the old man lives in me (Rom. 7); he is not wholly crucified, is not perfectly dead. He still lusts mightily against the Spirit, and stirs up inward wars, nor suffers the kingdom of the soul to be in peace.

But "Thou [that] rulest the raging of the sea: when the waves thereof arise, thou stillest them" (Ps. 89:9), arise and help me! "Scatter thou the people that delight in war" (Ps. 68:30); crush Thou them in Thy might. Display Thy wonderful works, I beseech Thee, and let Thy right hand be glorified; for there is no other hope or refuge for me, save in Thee, O Lord my God (Ps. 31:14).

Chapter 35

NO SECURITY FROM TEMPTATION

MY SON, you are never secure in this life, but as long as you live (Job 7:1) you need always spiritual armor. You dwell among enemies, and are fought against "on the right hand and on the left" (II Cor. 6:7).

If therefore you defend not yourself on every side with the shield of patience, you will not be long without a wound. Moreover, if you set not your heart fixedly on Me, with a sincere wish to suffer all things for Me, you will not be able to bear the heat of this combat, nor to attain to the palm of the blessed. You ought therefore manfully to go through all, and to use a strong hand against whatever withstands you.

For to him who overcomes is manna given (Rev. 2:17), and for the indolent there remains much misery.

If you seek rest in this life, how will you then attain to everlasting rest? Dispose not yourself for much rest, but for great patience. Seek true peace, not in earth, but in Heaven; not in men, nor in any other creature, but in God alone.

For the love of God you ought cheerfully to undergo all things; that is to say, labors and pains; temptations, vexations, anxieties, necessities, infirmities, injuries, slanders, reproofs, humiliations; confusions, corrections, and despisings. These are a help to virtue; these are the trial of a novice in Christ; these frame the heavenly crown. I will give an everlasting reward for a short labor, and infinite glory for transitory confusion.

Do you think that you shall always have spiritual consolations at your own will? My saints had not such always, but they had many afflictions, and sundry temptations, and great forsakings. Nevertheless in all these they bore themselves patiently, and trusted rather in God than in themselves; knowing "that the sufferings of this present time are not worthy to be compared with the glory that shall be revealed in us" (Rom. 8:18). Will you have that at once, which many after tears and great labors have hardly obtained?

"Wait on the Lord: be of good courage" (Ps. 27:14). Do not distrust, do not leave your place, but steadily expose both body and soul for the glory of God. I will reward you plenteously; "I will be with [you] in trouble" (Ps. 91:15).

Chapter 36

THE VAIN JUDGMENTS OF MEN

MY SON, cast your heart firmly on the Lord, and fear not the judgment of men, when conscience proves you holy and guiltless.

It is a good and happy thing to suffer in such a way; nor will this be grievous to a heart which is humble, and which trusts rather in God than in itself. Men say many things, and therefore little confidence is to be placed in them. Moreover, also, to satisfy all is not possible.

Although Paul endeavored to please all in the Lord, and was made "all things to all men" (I Cor. 9:22), yet he held it a very small thing that he should be judged of man's judgment (I Cor. 4:3). He did abundantly for the edification and salvation of others as much as lay in his power to do (Col. 1:29); yet he was by others sometimes judged, sometimes despised. Therefore he committed all to God, who knew all. Against the face of men who spoke unjust things, or thought vanities and lies, and boasted themselves as they listed, he defended himself, with humility and patience. Sometimes however he answered, lest for the weak his silence should prove a stumbling block (Acts 26; Phil. 1:14).

"Who art thou, that thou shouldest be afraid of a man that shall die" (Isa. 51:12)? Today he is, tomorrow he is not seen. Fear God, and you shall not shrink from the terrors of men. What power has any man over you by words or injuries? He hurts himself rather than you, nor shall he "escape the judgment of God" (Rom. 2:3). Keep God before your eyes, and contend not with peevish words. And though for the present you seem to be worsted, and to suffer shame, which you deserve not, do not therefore grieve, neither lessen your crown by impatience (Heb. 12:1, 2). But rather lift up your eyes to Me in Heaven, who am able to deliver you from all shame and wrong, and to "reward every man according to his works" (Matt. 16: 27; Rom. 2:6).

Chapter 37

RESIGNATION TO FREEDOM OF HEART

MY SON, forsake yourself, and you shall find Me (Matt. 16:24). Stand without choosing, and without any self-seeking; and you shall always gain. For even greater grace shall be added to you, the moment you resign yourself, provided you do not turn back to yourself again.

Lord, how often shall I resign myself? And wherein shall I forsake myself?

Always, and at every hour; in small things as well as in great. I except nothing, but in all things I will that you be found stripped. Otherwise, how can you be Mine, and I yours, unless you be stripped of all self-will both within and without? The sooner you do this, the better it will be with you; and the more fully and sincerely you do it, so much the more shall you please Me, and so much the greater shall be your gain.

Some there are who resign themselves, but with certain exceptions. They put not their full trust in God, and therefore they study how to provide for themselves. Some also at first offer all, but afterward being assailed with temptation, they return again to their own ways, and therefore make no progress in the path of virtue. These shall not attain to the true liberty of a pure heart, nor to the favor of sweet familiarity with Me, unless they first make an entire resignation and a daily sacrifice of themselves. Without this, no union that bears fruit stands firm nor shall stand.

I have very often said to you, and now again I say the same: Deny yourself (Matt. 16:24), resign yourself, and you shall enjoy great inward peace. Give all for all; ask for nothing, require back nothing; abide purely and unhesitatingly in Me, and you shall possess Me; you shall be free in heart, and darkness shall not cover you (Ps. 139:11). Let this be your endeavor, this your prayer, this your desire; that you may be stripped of all selfishness, and naked follow the naked Jesus; may die to self, and live eternally to Me. Then shall fail all vain imaginations, evil perturbations, and superfluous cares. Then also immoderate fear shall depart, and inordinate love shall die.

Chapter 38

GOOD GOVERNMENT, AND RECOURSE TO GOD IN DANGER

MY SON, you ought with all diligence to work toward this, that in every place, and in every external action or occupation, you may be inwardly free, and thoroughly master of yourself. That all things be under you, and not you under them; that you be lord and master of your own actions, not a slave or a hireling. Rather you should be as a freed man and a true Hebrew, passing over into the lot and freedom of the sons of God; who stand upon things present, and contemplate things eternal; who look on transitory things with the left eye, and with the right on the things of Heaven; whom temporal things draw not to cleave unto them. Rather they draw temporal things to serve them well, in such ways as they are ordained by God, and appointed by the great Work-master, who has left nothing in His creation without due order.

If too in every event you stand not on the outside,

nor with a carnal eye survey things seen or heard, but in every affair enter with Moses into the Tabernacle (Exod. 33:9) to ask counsel of the Lord, you shall sometimes hear the Divine Oracle, and shall return instructed concerning many things, both present and to come. For Moses always had recourse to the Tabernacle for the dissolving of doubts and questions, and fled to the help of prayer, for support under dangers and the iniquity of men. So ought you in like manner take refuge within the closet of your heart (Matt. 6:6), earnestly seeking the divine favor.

For we read, that for this cause Joshua and the children of Israel were deceived by the Gibeonites, because they "asked not counsel at the mouth of the Lord" (Josh. 9:14), but trusting too easily to sweet words were deluded by feigned piety.

Chapter 39

NOT FRETFUL IN BUSINESS

MY SON, commit your cause always to Me; I will dispose of it in due time. Wait for My ordering of it, and you shall find your good therefrom.

O Lord, most cheerfully do I commit all unto Thee, for my thinking can little avail. Would that I did not so much dwell on future events, but gave myself up without reluctance to Thy good pleasure.

My son, oftentimes a man vehemently struggles for something he desires, but when he has attained it, he changes his mind. For the affections remain not firmly around the same thing, but rather drive us from one thing to another. It is no small thing for a man to forsake himself even in things that are very small.

The true profiting of a man is the denying of himself; and a man who has denied himself is exceedingly free and secure. But the old Enemy (I Peter 5:8), who always sets himself against all who are good, ceases at no time from tempting, but day and night plots to cast the unwary headlong into the snare of deceit. "Watch and pray, that ye enter not into temptation" (Matt. 26:41), saith the Lord.

Chapter 40

MAN NO GOOD OF HIMSELF

WHAT IS MAN, that thou art mindful of him? Or the son of man, that thou visitest him" (Ps. 8:4)? What hath man deserved that Thou shouldest grant him Thy favor? O Lord, what cause can I have to complain, if Thou forsake me? Or if Thou do not that which I desire, what can I justly say against it? Surely this I may truly think and say: Lord, I am nothing, I can do nothing, I have nothing that is good of myself, but in all things I am falling away, and am ever tending to nothing. And unless Thou help me, and inwardly inform me, I become altogether lukewarm and ready to fall to pieces.

"But thou, O Lord, shalt endure forever" (Ps. 102:12); always good, just, and holy; doing all things well, justly, and holily, and ordering them in wisdom. Whereas I who am readier to go backward than forward do not always continue in one state, for "seven times" are passed over me (Dan. 4:16, 23, 32). Nevertheless it soon becomes better, when it so pleases Thee, and when Thou dost stretch forth Thy helping hand. For Thou canst help me alone without human aid, and so greatly strengthen me that my countenance shall be no more changed to sadness, but that in Thee alone shall my heart be turned and be at rest.

Wherefore, if I knew how to cast off all human consolation, either for the attainment of devotion, or because of my own necessities which enforce me to seek after Thee (for no mortal man can comfort me), then might I well hope in Thy grace, and rejoice in the gift of new consolation.

Thanks be unto Thee, from whom all comes, whenever it goes well with me.

But I am before Thee, vanity and nothing, a man unstable and weak. Whereof then can I glory? Or for what do I desire to be respected? Is it for being nothing? This too is most vain. Empty glory is in truth an evil pest, the greatest of vanities; because it draws from true glory, and robs of heavenly grace. For while a man pleases himself, he displeases Thee; while he seeks the praise of men, he is deprived of true virtues.

But true glory and holy exultation is to glory in Thee (Hab. 3:18) and not in himself; to rejoice in Thy name, not in his own virtue, nor to take delight in any creature except it be for Thy sake.

Praised be Thy name, not mine; magnified be Thy work, not mine; blessed be Thy holy name, but to me let no part of men's praises be given (Ps. 113:3; 115:1). Thou art my glory; Thou art the joy of my heart. In Thee will I glory and rejoice all the day, but yet of myself I will not glory, but in my infirmities (II Cor. 12:5).

Let the Jews seek the glory that comes of another (John 5:44), I will ask for that which comes from God alone. Truly all human glory, all temporal honor, all worldly exaltation, compared to Thy eternal glory, are vanity and folly. O my God, my Truth, and my Mercy, O blessed Trinity, to Thee alone be praise, honor, power and glory, throughout all ages, world without end!

Chapter 41

CONTEMPT OF ALL TEMPORAL HONOR

M Y SON, do not be concerned if you see others honored and exalted, but yourself condemned and debased. Lift up your heart to Me, and the contempt of men on earth shall not grieve you.

Lord, we are in blindness, and are quickly misled by vanity.

If I look rightly into myself, never has harm been done me by any creature; and therefore I cannot justly complain before Thee. But because I have often and grievously sinned against Thee, every creature justly takes arms against me. Unto me, therefore, shame and contempt are justly due, but unto Thee praise, honor, and glory.

And unless I prepare myself with cheerful willingness to be despised and forsaken of every creature, and to be esteemed entirely nothing, I cannot obtain inward peace and stability, nor be spiritually enlightened, nor be fully united unto Thee.

Chapter 42

OUR PEACE NOT SET ON MEN

My son, if you rest your peace on any person, because of your own feelings and because you live with him, you shall be unstable and entangled. But if you have recourse to the ever-living and abiding Truth, the desertion or death of a friend will not grieve you. Your love for your friend ought to be grounded in Me; and for My sake he is to be loved, whoever seems good to you, and is very dear to you in this life. Without Me friendship has no strength, nor shall endure; neither is that love true and pure which is not knit by Me.

You ought to be so dead to such affections toward beloved men, that (so far as you are concerned) you would choose to be without all human sympathy. The nearer man draws to God, the farther he retires from all earthly comfort. The higher also he ascends to God, the lower he descends in himself, and the meaner he is in his own sight. But he who attributes any good to himself, hinders God's grace from coming to him; because the grace of the Holy Spirit ever seeks a humble heart (I Peter 5:5). If you could but bring yourself to nothing, and empty yourself of all created love, then ought I with great grace to overflow into you. When you look to the creature, the countenance of the Creator is withdrawn. Learn in all things to overcome yourself for the sake of your Creator; then you shall have power to attain to divine knowledge. How little is anything, if it is inordinately loved and regarded, if it keeps you away from the Highest, and corrupts the soul.

Chapter 43

AGAINST VAIN AND WORLDLY KNOWLEDGE

M Y SON, let not the fair and subtle sayings of men move you. "For the kingdom of God is not in word, but in power" (I Cor. 4:20). Give heed to My words, which kindle the heart, and enlighten the mind; they produce contrition, and they supply manifold consolation.

Never read a word, that you may appear more learned. Be studious for the mortification of your sins; for this will profit more than the knowledge of many hard questions. When you shall have read and learned many things, you must needs return to one beginning.

I am "he that teacheth man knowledge" (Ps. 94:10), and I bestow on little children a clearer understanding than can be taught by man. He to whom I speak shall quickly be wise, and shall profit much in the Spirit. Woe be to them who inquire many curious things of men, and care little about the way of serving Me! The time will come, when the Master of masters, Christ the Lord of angels, shall appear, to examine the consciences of everyone. And then will He "search Jerusalem with candles," and "the hidden things of darkness" shall be laid open (Zeph. 1:12; I Cor. 4:5), and men's tongues shall be silent.

I am He who in one instant do lift up the humble mind to comprehend more reasonings of eternal truth, than if one had studied ten years in the schools.

I teach without noise of words, without confusion of opinions, without the pride of honor, without the scuffling of arguments.

I am He who instructs men to despise earthly things, to loath things present, to seek things eternal, to relish things eternal; to flee honors, to endure offenses, to place all hope in Me, out of Me to desire nothing, and above all things ardently to love Me. For a certain one, by loving Me from his heart, learned things divine, and was wont to speak marvelous things. He profited more by forsaking all things than by studying subtleties.

Nevertheless, to some men, I speak common things, to others things special. To some I show Myself sweetly in signs and figures, while to some I reveal mysteries in much light. The voice of books is one, but it informs not all alike. Inwardly I am the teacher, the truth, the searcher of the heart, the discerner of thoughts, the promoter of actions, distributing to every man as I shall judge meet.

Chapter 44

NOT DRAWING TROUBLE FROM OUTWARD THINGS

My son, in many things it is your duty to be ignorant, and to esteem yourself as one dead upon the earth, and to "whom the world is crucified" (Gal. 4:14). There are many things too which it is your duty to pass by with a deaf ear, and be rather mindful of those which belong to peace. It is more profitable to turn away one's eyes from things that displease, and to leave to each person his own opinion, than to wait upon contentious discourses. If you stand well with God, and regard His judgment, you shall very easily endure defeat.

O Lord, to what a pass are we come! Behold, we bewail a temporal loss; for a pitiful gain we toil and run; while spiritual harm passes away into forgetfulness, and hardly at last do we return to a sense of it. That which little or nothing profits is minded, and that which is especially needful is negligently passed over. Because the whole man slides away to things external, and unless he speedily come to himself, he willingly lies sunk in outward things.

Chapter 45

CREDIT NOT GIVEN TO ALL, AND MAN PRONE TO OFFEND IN WORDS

GIVE US HELP from trouble: for vain is the help of man" (Ps. 60:11). How often have I failed with faithfulness there, where I thought I possessed it! How often too have I found it there, where beforehand I least expected it! Vain therefore is hope in men; but the salvation of the righteous is in Thee, O God! Blessed be Thou, O Lord my God, in all things that befall us!

Weak are we and unstable; quickly are we deceived and altogether changed. Who is the man who is able in all things so warily and circumspectly to keep himself, as never to come into any deception or perplexity? But he who trusts in Thee, O Lord, and seeks Thee with a single heart, does not so easily slip (Prov. 10:29). And if he fall into any tribulation, be he ever so much entangled, yet shall he quickly through Thee be drawn out, or by Thee be comforted; for Thou wilt not forsake him who hopes in Thee to the end.

Rare is a faithful friend who continues in all his friend's distresses. Thou, O Lord, Thou alone art most faithful at all times, and beside Thee there is none other like unto Thee.

How wise was that holy soul which said: "My mind is firmly settled, and is grounded in Christ"! If thus it were with me, the fear of man would not so easily vex me, nor darts of words move me.

Who is sufficient to foresee, who to guard against, all future evils? If even things that are foreseen oftentimes hurt us, how can unforeseen evils otherwise than grievously smite us? But wretch as I am, why have I not foreseen better for myself? Why too have I so easily given credit to others? But we are men, nothing else are we but frail men, even though by many we are reputed and called angels.

Whom shall I trust, O Lord? Whom but Thee? Thou art the truth, who deceivest not nor canst be deceived. And on the other side, "every man [is] a liar" (Rom. 3:4), weak, inconstant, and subject to fall, especially in words. Therefore we must scarcely ever immediately give credit to that which on the face of it seems to sound right.

How wisely hast Thou warned us to beware of men; and that "a man's enemies are the men of his own house" (Micah 7:6); and not to believe if one should say, "Lo, here . . . or there" (Matt. 24:23).

I have been taught by my own hurt, and I would it may make me more cautious, and not more unwise. "Be wary," saith one, "be wary, keep to thyself what I say to thee." And while I keep silence, and think it is secret, he cannot himself keep that which he desired me to keep, but presently betrays both me and himself, and is gone.

From such tales and heedless persons protect me,

O Lord, that I neither fall into their hands, nor ever commit such things myself. Give the word of truth and steadfastness to my mouth, and remove from me a crafty tongue. What I am not willing to suffer, I ought by all means to beware of doing.

Oh, how good it is and tending to peace, to be silent about other men, and not to believe indifferently all that is said, nor too easily to tell it further (Prov. 25:9). To lay oneself open to few; and ever to be seeking after Thee as the searcher of the heart (Isa. 26:3); and not to be carried about with every wind of words. But to desire that all things both within and without be accomplished according to the pleasure of Thy will!

How safe is it, for the keeping of heavenly grace, to avoid estimation of men, and not to seek those things which seem to cause admiration abroad; but to pursue with all diligence the things which bring amendment of life and godly zeal! How many has virtue harmed, by being known and too hastily commended! How truly profitable has grace been when preserved in silence in this frail life, which we are told is all temptation and warfare!

Chapter 46

WHEN THE ARROWS OF
WORDS ASSAIL

M Y SON, stand steadily, and put your trust in Me
(Ps. 37:3); for what are words, but words? They
fly through the air, but they cannot hurt a stone. If you
are guilty, gladly improve yourself; if you are conscious
of no fault, consider that you would gladly endure this
for God's sake (I Peter 2:19, 20). It is little enough
that sometimes you should endure even words, since
you have not yet the courage to bear hard stripes.

And why do such small matters affect you? Because you are yet carnal (I Cor. 3:3), and regard men
more than you ought. It is because you are afraid of
being despised, that you are unwilling to be reproved
for faults, and cover up with excuses. But look within
and you shall acknowledge that the world is yet alive
in you, and a vain desire to please men. For when you
shrink from being abased and confounded for your
failings, it is evident surely that you are neither truly
humble, nor truly dead to the world, nor is the world
crucified to you.

But hear My Word, and you shall not care for ten
thousand words of men. Behold, if all should be
spoken against you that could be most maliciously

invented, what would it hurt you, if you would suffer it to pass entirely away and make no more reckoning of it than a mote? Could it pluck so much as one hair from your head (Luke 12:7)?

But he who has no heart within him, nor has God before his eyes, is easily moved with a word of dispraise. Whereas he who trusts in Me, and has no wish to stand by his own judgment, shall be free from the fear of men. For I am the Judge (Ps. 7:8) and the discerner of all secrets. I well understand how the matter passed; I know him who offered the injury, and him that suffered it. From Me proceeded that word; by My permission this has happened; "that the thoughts of many hearts may be revealed" (Luke 2:35). I shall judge the guilty, and the innocent; but by a secret judgment I have thought fit beforehand to prove them both. The testimony of men oftentimes deceives. My judgment is true; it shall stand, and shall not be overthrown. It commonly lies hidden, and is manifest but to few in every matter; yet it never errs, nor can err, although to the eyes of the foolish it may seem not right.

Therefore men ought to come to me in every judgment; not to lean on their own opinions. For the just man will not be disturbed (Prov. 12:13), whatever befalls him from God. Even if an unjust charge be brought against him, he will not care. Nor again will he vainly exult, if through others he be justly vindicated. For he considers that I am He who "trieth the hearts and reins" (Ps. 7:9), who judge not according to the outward face and human appearance. Oftentimes that is found worthy of blame in My sight, which in the judgment of men is thought worthy of praise.

O Lord God, the just Judge, strong and patient, Thou who knowest the frailty and wickedness of men, be Thou my strength, and all my confidence, for my own conscience suffices me not. Thou knowest what I know not; and therefore I ought to humble myself under all blame and to bear it meekly. Of Thy mercy then forgive me whenever I have acted otherwise, and grant me once more the grace of more thorough endurance. Because better to me is Thine overflowing pity for the obtaining of pardon, than my own fancied righteousness to ward off the secret misgivings of conscience. Although I know nothing against myself, yet I cannot hereby justify myself (I Cor. 4:4); for without Thy mercy, "in thy sight shall no man living be justified" (Ps. 143:2).

Chapter 47

GRIEVOUS THINGS ENDURED

M Y SON, be not wearied by the labors which you have undertaken for my sake, nor let tribulations cast you down. But let My promise strengthen and comfort you under every circumstance. I am well able to reward you, above all measure and degree.

You shall not long toil here, nor always be oppressed with griefs. Wait a little while, and you shall see a speedy end of your evils. There will come an hour when all labor and tumult shall cease. Poor and brief is all that which passes away with time.

Do in earnest what you do; labor faithfully in My vineyard (Matt. 20:7); I will be your recompense. Write, read, chant, mourn, keep silence, pray, endure crosses manfully. Life everlasting is worth all these battles, and greater than these. Peace shall come in one day which is known unto the Lord, and there shall be "not day, nor night" (Zech. 14:7) (that is, of this present time), but unceasing light, infinite brightness, steadfast peace, and secure rest. Then you shall not say: "Who shall deliver me from the body of this death?" (Rom. 7:24); nor cry: "Woe is me, that I sojourn in Mesech" (Ps. 120:5). For death shall be cast down headlong, and there shall be salvation which can never fail, no more anxiety, blessed joy, companionship sweet and noble.

Oh, if you had seen the everlasting crowns of the saints in Heaven, and with what great glory they now rejoice, who once were esteemed by this world as contemptible, and in a manner unworthy of life itself! Truly you would humble yourself even to the earth, and would rather seek to be under all than to have command even over one. Neither would you long for this life's pleasant days, but rather would rejoice to suffer affliction for God, and esteem it your greatest gain to be reputed as nothing among men. Oh, if these things had a sweet savor to you, and pierced to the bottom of your heart, how could you dare so much as once to complain!

Lift up your face therefore to Heaven. Behold, I and all My saints with Me, who in this world had great conflict, do now rejoice, now are comforted, now secure, now at rest, and shall remain with Me everlastingly in the kingdom of My Father!

Chapter 48

DAY OF ETERNITY, AND LIFE'S RESTRICTIONS

O BLESSED MANSION of the city which is above (Rev. 21:2)! O day of eternity, which night obscures not, but the highest truth ever enlightens! O day ever joyful, ever secure, and never changing to the opposite! Oh, that that day had shone upon us, and that all these temporal things were at an end! To the saints indeed it shines glorious with perpetual brightness, but only afar off, and as "through a glass" (I Cor. 13: 12), to those who are pilgrims on the earth. The citizens of Heaven know how full of gladness is that day, but "the banished sons of Eve" bewail the bitterness and tediousness of this.

The days of this life are few and evil (Job 7), full of sorrows and restrictions. Here a man is defiled with many sins, ensnared with many passions, held fast by many fears, racked with many cares, distracted with many curiosities, entangled with many vanities, compassed about with many errors, worn away with many labors, burdened with temptations, enervated by pleasures, tormented with want.

Oh, when shall be the end of these evils? When shall I be mindful, O Lord, of Thee alone (Ps. 71: 16)? When to the full shall I rejoice in Thee? When shall I be without all hindrance in true liberty, without all heaviness of mind and body? When shall I have solid peace, peace secure and undisturbed, peace within and peace without, peace every way assured? O Jesus, when shall I stand to behold Thee? When shall I contemplate the glory of Thy kingdom? When wilt Thou be unto me all in all? Oh, when shall I be with Thee in Thy kingdom, which Thou hast prepared for Thy beloved ones from all eternity?

I am left, a poor and banished man, in the land of mine enemies where there are daily wars and great calamities.

Comfort my banishment, assuage my sorrow; for my whole desire sighs after Thee. For all is a burden to me, whatever this world offers for consolation. I long to enjoy Thee most inwardly, but I cannot attain unto it. I desire to cling fast to things heavenly, but temporal things and unmortified passions weigh me down. With the mind I wish to be above all things, but with the flesh I am enforced against my will to be beneath them. Thus, unhappy man that I am (Rom. 7:24; 8:23), I fight against myself, and am become grievous to myself, while my spirit seeks to be above, and my flesh to be below. Oh, what do I inwardly suffer, while in my mind I dwell on things heavenly, and presently while I pray, a multitude of fleshly things hasten upon me!

"O God, be not far from me: O my God, make haste for my help" (Ps. 71:12). "Cast forth lightning, and scatter them: shoot out thine arrows" (Ps. 146:6), and let all the imaginations of the Enemy be confounded. Gather in, and call home my senses unto Thee; make me to forget all worldly things; grant me to cast away speedily and to scorn all sinful phantoms. Succor me, O Thou eternal Truth, that no vanity may move me! Come to me, Thou heavenly sweetness, and let all impurity flee from before Thy face.

Pardon me also, and in mercy deal gently with me, as in prayer I think on aught beside Thee.

For truly I confess, that I am wont to be exceedingly distracted. For oftentimes I am not where I am bodily standing or sitting; but rather I am where my thoughts carry me. Where my thoughts are, there am I; and commonly there are my thoughts, where my affection is. That readily hastens to me, which naturally brings delight, or by custom is pleasing. And for this cause, Thou that art truth itself hast plainly said: "For where your treasure is, there will your heart be also" (Matt. 6:21). If I love Heaven, I willingly muse on heavenly things. If I love the world, I rejoice with the felicity of the world, and grieve for the adversity thereof. If I love the flesh, I constantly imagine those things that belong to the flesh. If I love the Spirit, I delight to think on things spiritual. For whatever things I love, of these do I willingly speak and hear, and carry home with me the forms thereof.

But blessed is the man who for Thy sake, O Lord, grants leave to depart unto all creatures, who does violence to his nature, and through fervor of the Spirit crucifies the lusts of the flesh; that with a serene conscience he may offer a pure prayer unto Thee, and all earthly things both outwardly and inwardly being excluded, he may be admitted into the heavenly choirs.

Chapter 49

DESIRE OF ETERNAL LIFE, AND REWARDS PROMISED

MY SON, when you perceive the desire of eternal bliss to be poured from above, and long to depart out of the tabernacle of the body, that you may be able to contemplate My brightness, without shadow of turning, open your heart wide, and receive this holy inspiration with your whole desire. Give full thanks to the heavenly Father who treats you with such condescension, visits you mercifully, stirs you up fervently, sustains you powerfully, lest through your own weight you sink down to earthly things. For you do not obtain this by your own thought or endeavor, but by the mere condescension of heavenly grace and divine regard; to the end that you may make further progress in all virtues, and in greater humility, and prepare yourself for future conflicts, and may earnestly strive to cleave unto Me with the whole affection of your heart, and to serve Me with a fervent will.

My son, oftentimes the fire burns, but the flame ascends not up without smoke. So likewise the desires of some men burn toward heavenly things, and yet they are not free from temptation of carnal affection. And therefore they act not altogether purely for the honor of God, in that they make such earnest requests to Him.

Such also oftentimes is your desire, which you have pretended to be so earnest. For that is not pure and perfect, which is tinctured with self-seeking. Ask not for that which is delightful and profitable to you, but for that which is acceptable to Me, and tends to My honor. For if you judge aright, you ought to prefer and follow My appointment, rather than your own desire, or anything that is desired.

I know your desire, and have heard your many groanings. Already you will to be in "the glorious liberty of the children of God" (Rom. 8:21). Already you delight in the everlasting habitation, and the heavenly country which is full of joy. But that hour is not yet come. There remains still another time, and that a time of war, a time of labor and of trial. You desire to be filled with the chiefest good, but you cannot attain it at once. "I am" (John 8:58); wait for Me (saith the Lord) "until the kingdom of God shall come" (Luke 22:18).

You are still to be tried upon earth, and to be exercised in many things. Comfort shall be sometimes given, but the abundant fullness thereof is not granted. "Only be thou strong and very courageous" (Josh. 1:7), in doing as well as in suffering things contrary to nature.

It is your duty to "put on the new man" (Eph. 4: 24), and to be changed into another person (I Sam. 10:6). It is your duty oftentimes to do what you would not; and what you would do, it is your duty to leave.

That which pleases others shall prosper; that which pleases you shall not prosper. That which others say shall be heard; what you say shall be accounted nothing. Others shall ask and shall receive; you shall ask but shall not obtain. Others shall be great in the sight of men, but about you there shall be silence. To others this or that shall be committed, but you shall be accounted useful for nought. At this nature will sometimes be troubled, and it is a great thing if you bear it with silence. In these and many like instances, the faithful servant of the Lord is wont to be tried, how far he can deny and in all things break himself.

There is scarcely anything in which you have such need to die to yourself, as in seeing and suffering those things that are adverse to your will; especially when that is commanded to be done which seems inconvenient, or useless. And because you are under authority you dare not resist the higher power, therefore it seems hard to walk at another's nod, and to give up your own opinion.

But consider, My son, the fruit of these labors, the

end coming swiftly, and the reward exceedingly great; and you will not have heaviness from these things, but the strongest comfort of your patience. For instead of that little of your will which you now so readily forsake, you shall always have your will in Heaven. There surely you shall find all that you may wish, all that you shall desire. There you shall have within your reach all good without fear of losing it. There shall your will be ever one with Me; it shall not covet any outward or private thing. There none shall withstand you, no man shall complain of you, no man hinder you, nothing come in your way. But all things you desire shall be there, and refresh your affection, and fill it up to the brim. There I will give you glory for the reproach which you suffered here, "the garment of praise for the spirit of heaviness" (Isa. 61:3), for the lowest place a kingly throne forever. There shall the fruit of obedience appear, the labor of repentance shall rejoice, and humble subjection shall be gloriously crowned.

At present then, bend yourself humbly under the hands of all, and care not who said this or commanded it. But take special care, that whether your superior, inferior, or equal, requires anything of you, or hints at anything, take it all in good part, and with a sincere will endeavor to fulfill it. Let one seek this, another that; let this man glory in this, the other in that, and be praised a thousand times. But rejoice neither in this, nor in that, but in your own contempt, and in the good pleasure and honor of Me alone. This is what you are to wish, that "whether it be by life, or by death," God may be always glorified in you (Phil. 1:20).

Chapter 50

A DESOLATE MAN OUGHT TO OFFER HIMSELF INTO THE HANDS OF GOD

O LORD GOD, holy Father, be Thou blessed both now and forevermore, because as Thou wilt, so it is done, and what Thou doest is good. Let Thy servant rejoice in Thee, not in himself nor in anything else. Thou alone art the true gladness, Thou art my hope and my crown, Thou art my joy and my honor, O Lord. What has Thy servant, but what he has received from Thee (I Cor. 4:7), even without any merit of his own? Thine are all things, which Thou hast given, and which Thou hast made.

"I am afflicted and ready to die from my youth up" (Ps. 88:15), and my soul is sorrowful sometimes even unto tears; sometimes also my spirit is disquieted, by reason of impending sufferings. I long after the joy of peace; the peace of Thy children I earnestly crave, who are fed by Thee in the light of Thy consolation. If Thou give peace, if Thou pour into me holy joy, the soul of Thy servant shall be full of melody, and devout in Thy praise. But if Thou withdraw Thyself (as very often Thou art wont), Thy servant will not be able to "run the way of thy commandments" (Ps. 119:32). Rather he will bow his knees, and smite his breast, because it is not now as it was in times past, when Thy candle shined upon his head (Job 29:3), and "under the shadow of thy wings" (Ps. 17:8) he was protected from the temptations which assaulted him.

O righteous Father, and ever to be praised, the hour is come that Thy servant is to be tested. O beloved Father, meet and right it is that in this hour Thy servant should suffer something for Thy sake. O Father, evermore to be honored, the hour is come, which from all eternity Thou didst foreknow should come; that for a short time Thy servant should outwardly be oppressed, but inwardly should ever live with Thee. Let him be for a little while held in contempt, and humbled, and fail in the sight of men; be wasted with sufferings and languors; that he may rise again with Thee in the morning dawn of the new light, and be glorified in Heaven.

Holy Father, Thou hast so appointed it, and hast so willed; and that is fulfilled which Thou hast commanded. For this is a favor to Thy friend, for Thy love to suffer and be afflicted in the world by whom and as often as Thou permit it to befall him. Without Thy counsel and providence and without cause, nothing is done in the earth. "It is good for me, that I have been afflicted" (Ps. 119:71), that I may learn Thy righteous judgments, and may cast away all haughtiness of heart, and all presumptuousness. It is profitable for me, that "shame hath covered my face" (Ps. 69:7), that I may seek Thee for consolation rather than men. I have learned also hereby to dread Thy unsearchable judgment, who afflictest the just with the wicked, though not without equity and justice.

I give Thee thanks, for that Thou hast not spared my sins, but hast worn me down with bitter stripes, inflicting sorrows and sending afflictions upon me within and without. There is none else under Heaven who can comfort me, but Thou only, O Lord my God, the heavenly Physician of souls, who strikes and heals, who brings down to Hell and back again (Ps. 18:16). Thy discipline is over me, and Thy rod shall instruct me.

Behold, O beloved Father, I am in Thy hands; under the rod of Thy correction I bow myself! Smite my back and my neck, that I may bend my crookedness to Thy will. Make me a dutiful and humble disciple, as Thou art wont to be kind, that I may walk at Thy every nod. Unto Thee I commend myself, and all that is mine, to be corrected. It is better to be punished here than hereafter.

Thou knowest all things generally, and in particular, and there is nothing hidden from Thee in man's conscience. Before things are done, Thou knowest that they will come to pass; and Thou hast no need that any should teach or admonish Thee of what is going on here on the earth. Thou knowest what is expedient for my profit, and how greatly tribulation serves to scour off the rust of sins. Do with me, according to Thy desired good pleasure, and disdain me not for my sinful life, known to none so well and clearly as to Thee alone.

Grant me, O Lord, to know that which is worth knowing, to love that which is worth loving, to praise that which pleases Thee most, to esteem that which to Thee seems precious, to abhor that which in Thy sight is unclean.

Suffer me not to judge according to the sight of the outward eyes, nor to give sentence according to the hearing of the ears of ignorant men (Isa. 11:3); but with a true judgment to discern between things visible and spiritual, and above all to be ever searching after the good pleasure of Thy will. The minds of men are often deceived in their judgments; the lovers of the world too are deceived in loving only visible things. What does a man gain for being by man esteemed great? The deceitful in extolling the deceitful plays him false, the vain man the vain, the blind man the blind, the weak man the weak; and in truth rather puts him to shame, while he vainly praises him. "For what every one is in Thy sight, so much is he, and no more," said a humble servant.

Chapter 51

WORKS OF HUMILITY

M Y SON, you are not able always to stand in the more fervent desire of virtue, nor to persist in the highest stage of contemplation. But you must sometimes by reason of original corruption descend to inferior things, and bear the burden of this corruptible life, though against your will and with weariness. As long as you carry a mortal body, you shall feel weariness and heaviness of heart. You ought therefore in the flesh oftentimes to bewail the burden of the flesh; for you cannot employ yourself unceasingly in spiritual studies and divine contemplation.

Then it is expedient to flee to humble and outward works, and to refresh yourself with good actions; to expect with a firm confidence My coming and heavenly visitation; to bear banishment patiently and dryness of mind, till again you are visited by Me, and set free from all anxieties. For I will cause you to forget painful toils, and thoroughly to enjoy inward quietness. I will spread open before you the pleasant fields of the Scriptures, that with an enlarged heart you may begin to "run the way of [my] commandments" (Ps. 119:32). And you shall say: "The sufferings of this present time are not worthy to be compared with the glory which shall be revealed in us" (Rom. 8:18).

195

Chapter 52

UNWORTHY OF COMFORT,
DESERVING OF STRIPES

O LORD, I am not worthy of Thy consolation, nor of any spiritual visitation; and therefore Thou dealest justly with me, when Thou leavest me poor and desolate. For though I could shed a sea of tears, still I should not be worthy of Thy consolation. I am not then worthy of anything but to be scourged and punished; because grievously and often I have offended Thee, and in many things have greatly sinned. Wherefore, when the true reason is weighed, I am not worthy even of the least consolation.

But Thou, O gracious and merciful God, who willest not that Thy works should perish, to "make known the riches of his glory on the vessels of mercy" (Rom. 9:23), vouchsafest even beyond all his desert to comfort Thy servant above the manner of men. For Thy consolations are not like the communings of men.

What have I done, O Lord, that Thou shouldest bestow any heavenly comfort upon me? I remember that I have done naught of good, but that I have been always prone to sin, and slow to amendment. This is true, and I cannot deny it. If I should say otherwise,

Thou wouldest stand against me (Job 9:2, 3), and there would be none to defend me. What have I deserved for my sins, but Hell and everlasting fire? I confess in very truth that I am worthy of all scorn and contempt, nor is it fit that I should be remembered among Thy devout servants. And although I be unwilling to hear this, yet I will for the truth's sake lay open my sins, even against myself, that I may be the more readily accounted worthy to obtain Thy mercy. What shall I say, in that I am guilty, and full of all confusion? My mouth can utter nothing but this word only: I have sinned, O Lord! I have sinned, pardon me, have mercy on me (Ps. 51). Suffer me a little "that I may take comfort a little, before I go . . . to the land of darkness and the shadow of death" (Job 10:20, 21).

What dost Thou so much require of a guilty and miserable sinner, except that he be contrite and that he humble himself for his offenses? Of true contrition and humbling of heart is born hope of forgiveness; the troubled conscience is reconciled; the grace which was lost is recovered; man is preserved from the wrath to come; and God and the penitent soul meet together with a holy kiss. Humble contrition for sins is an acceptable sacrifice unto Thee, O Lord (Ps. 51:17), giving forth a savor far sweeter in Thy sight than the perfume of frankincense. This is also the pleasant ointment (Luke 7:38), which Thou wouldest should be poured upon Thy sacred feet; for "a broken and a contrite heart, O God, Thou wilt not despise" (Ps. 51:17). Here is the place of refuge from the face of the

Enemy's anger. Here is amended and washed away whatever defilement has been anywhere else contracted.

Chapter 53

THE GRACE OF GOD APART FROM EARTHLY THINGS

M Y SON, My grace is precious; it suffers not itself to be mingled with external things, nor with earthly consolations. You ought therefore to cast away all the hindrances of grace, if you desire to receive the inpouring thereof.

Seek a secret place, love to dwell alone, desire the conversation of none; but rather pour out devout prayer to God, that you may keep a contrite mind and a pure conscience. Esteem the whole world as nothing; prefer waiting upon God before all outward things. For you will not be able to wait upon Me, and at the same time take delight in transitory things. It is meet that you remove yourself from acquaintances and dear friends (Matt. 19:29), and keep your mind void of all temporal comfort. The apostle Peter beseeches that the faithful of Christ keep themselves in this world "as strangers and pilgrims" (I Peter 2:11).

What great confidence shall he have at the hour of death, whom no affection to anything detains in the world! But what it is to have a heart so separate from all things, the sickly mind does not as yet comprehend; nor does the natural man know the liberty of the spiritual man. Notwithstanding if he would be truly spiritual he ought to renounce those who are far off, as well as those who are near to him, and to beware of no man more than of himself. If you perfectly overcome yourself you shall very easily bring all else under the yoke. The perfect victory is to triumph over ourselves. For he who keeps himself subject, that his sensual affections be obedient to reason, and his reason in all things obedient to Me, that person is truly conqueror of himself, and lord of the world.

If you desire to mount to this height, you must begin like a man, and lay the axe to the root (Matt. 3: 10), that you may pluck up and destroy the hidden inordinate inclination to self, and to all private and earthly good.

By this fault (that a man too inordinately loves himself) almost everything is upheld, which ought from its roots to be overcome. If this evil be once vanquished and subdued, there will presently ensue great peace and tranquility. But because few labor to be perfectly dead to themselves, or fully go forth from themselves, therefore in themselves they remain entangled, nor can be lifted up in spirit above themselves.

But he who desires to walk at liberty (Ps. 119:45) with Me must mortify all corrupt and inordinate affections, and should not with desire cleave to any creature in selfish love.

Chapter 54

NATURE AND GRACE

M Y SON, mark diligently the motions of human nature and of divine grace. For they move in a very contrary and subtle manner, and can hardly be distinguished but by him who is spiritual and inwardly enlightened. All men indeed desire that which is good, and pretend somewhat good in their words and deeds; and therefore under the show of good many are deceived.

Nature is crafty, and draws away many, ensnares and deceives them, and always has self for its end. But grace walks in simplicity, abstains from all show of evil, shelters not itself under deceits, does all things purely for God's sake, in whom also it finally rests.

Nature is loath to die, or to be kept down, or to be overcome, or to be in subjection, or readily to be subdued. But grace studies self-mortification, resists sensuality, seeks to be in subjection, longs to be defeated, has no wish to use its own liberty. It loves to be kept under discipline, and desires not to rule over any, but under God to live, to stand, and to be, and for His sake it is ready humbly "to submit to every ordinance of man" (I Peter 2:13).

Nature strives for its own advantage, and considers

what profit it may reap by another. Grace considers not what is profitable and useful to itself, but rather what may be for the good of many (I Cor. 10:33).

Nature willingly receives honor and reverence, but grace faithfully assigns all honor and glory to God.

Nature fears shame and contempt, but grace rejoices to suffer shame for His name (Acts 5:41).

Nature loves leisure and bodily rest; grace cannot be unemployed, but cheerfully embraces labor.

Nature seeks to have things that are curious and beautiful, and abhors those which are cheap and coarse. But grace delights in what is plain and humble, despises not rough things, nor refuses to be clad in that which is old and patched.

Nature respects temporal things, rejoices at earthly gains, sorrows for loss, is irritated by every slight word of injury. But grace looks to things eternal, cleaves not to things temporal (II Cor. 4:18), is not disturbed at losses, nor soured with hard words; because it has placed its treasure and joy in Heaven (Matt. 6:20) where nothing perishes.

Nature is covetous, more willingly receives than gives, and loves to have things private and its own. But grace is kind and openhearted, shuns private interest, is content with a few things, judges that "it is more blessed to give than to receive" (Acts 20:35).

Nature inclines a man to the creatures, to his own flesh, to vanities, and to rovings about. But grace draws to God and to virtues; renounces creatures, avoids the world, hates the desires of the flesh, restrains wanderings abroad, blushes to be seen in public.

Nature is willing to have some outward solace, wherein it may be sensibly delighted. But grace seeks consolation in God alone, and to have delight in the highest good above all visible things.

Nature manages everything for its own gain and profit. It cannot without payment do anything, but for every kindness hopes to obtain either what is equal, or what is better, or at least praise or favor, and to have its works and gifts and words much valued. But grace seeks no temporal thing, nor desires any other reward than God alone for wages, nor asks more of temporal necessities, except so far as these may serve for the obtaining of things eternal.

Nature rejoices to have many friends and kinsfolk. It glories in noble place and noble birth, smiles on the powerful, fawns on the rich, applauds those like itself. But grace loves even enemies, and is not puffed up with multitude of friends; nor thinks aught of place or of high birth, unless there shall be the greater virtue. It favors the poor rather than the rich, sympathizes more with the innocent than with the powerful, rejoices with the true man, not with the deceitful. It is ever exhorting good men "to covet earnestly the best gifts" (I Cor. 12:31), and by virtues to become like to the Son of God.

Nature quickly complains of want and of trouble; grace with constancy endures need.

Nature turns all things back to itself, strives and argues for itself. But grace brings back all things to God, from where originally they flowed. It ascribes no good to itself, nor does it arrogantly presume; it contends not, nor prefers its own opinion before others. But in every matter of sense and understanding it submits itself to the eternal wisdom and the divine judgment.

Nature is eager to know secrets and to hear news; likes to appear abroad, and to make proof of many things by its own senses. It desires to be acknowledged, and to do things for which it may be praised and admired. But grace cares not to hear news, nor curious matters, because all this takes its rise from the old corruption of man; seeing that upon earth there is nothing new, nothing durable. Grace teaches therefore to restrain the senses, to shun vain self-pleasing and outward show, humbly to hide those things that are worthy of admiration and praise, and from every matter and in every knowledge to seek profitable fruit, and the praise and honor of God. It will not have itself publicly proclaimed, but desires that God should be blessed in His gifts, who out of mere love bestows all things.

This grace is a supernatural light, and a special gift of God, and the proper mark of the elect, and pledge of everlasting salvation. It raises up a man from earthly things to love the things of Heaven, and from being carnal makes him a spiritual man.

The more therefore nature is pressed down and subdued, so much the greater grace is poured in. And every day by new visitations the inward man becomes reformed according to the image of God.

Chapter 55

CORRUPTION OF NATURE; EFFICACY OF DIVINE GRACE

O LORD, MY GOD, who hast created me after Thine own image and likeness (Gen. 1:26), grant me this grace, which Thou hast showed to be so great and so necessary to salvation; that I may overcome my evil nature, which draws me to sin and to perdition. For I feel in my flesh the law of sin "warring against the law of my mind" (Rom. 7:23), and leading me captive to the obeying of sensuality in many things. Neither can I resist the passions thereof, unless Thy grace fervently infused into my heart assists me.

There is need of Thy grace, yea, of great grace, that nature may be overcome, which "is evil from his youth" (Gen. 8:21). For through the first man, Adam, nature being fallen and corrupted by sin, the penalty of this stain has descended upon all mankind, so that nature itself, which by Thee was created good and upright, is now represented as the sin and infirmity of corrupted nature; because the inclination thereof left to itself draws to evil and to lower things. For the small power which remains is as it were a spark lying hidden in the ashes. This is natural reason itself, encompassed about with great darkness, yet retaining the discernment of good and evil, the difference between true and false, although it be unable to fulfill all that it approves, and enjoys no longer the full light of the truth, nor soundness of its own affections.

Hence it is, O my God, that "I delight in the law of God after the inward man" (Rom. 7:22), knowing Thy commandment to be good, just, and holy, proving also that all evil and sin are to be shunned. But with the flesh I serve the law of sin, while I obey sensuality rather than reason.

Therefore "to will is present with me; but how to perform that which is good I find not" (Rom. 7:18).

I often purpose many good things, but because grace is wanting to help my infirmity, upon a light resistance, I fail.

And it comes to pass that I know the way of perfection, and see clearly enough how I ought to act; but being pressed down with the weight of my own corruption, I do not attain what is more perfect.

O Lord, how entirely needful is Thy grace for me, to begin anything good, to proceed with it, and to accomplish it. For without it I can do nothing (John 15:5), but in Thee I can do all things, when Thy grace strengthens me (Phil. 4:13).

O grace, truly celestial! Without it our own worthy actions are nothing, nor are any gifts of nature to be esteemed. Neither arts nor riches, neither beauty nor strength, neither wit nor eloquence, avail before Thee, without Thy grace, O Lord. For gifts of nature are common to good and bad, but the peculiar gift of the elect is grace and love; and they that are blessed therewith are accounted worthy of everlasting life. So eminent is this grace, that neither the gift of prophecy, nor the working of miracles, nor any speculation is of any esteem without it. No, not even faith or hope, or any other virtues, are unto Thee acceptable without love and grace (I Cor. 13:13).

Grace makes the poor in spirit rich in virtues, and renders him who is rich in many goods humble in heart. Come Thou down to me, O Lord, come and in the morning fill me with Thy comfort, lest my soul faint for weariness and dryness of mind!

I beseech Thee, O Lord, that I may find grace in Thy sight; for "thy grace is sufficient for [me]" (II Cor. 12:9), though other things that nature longs for are not obtained. Although I am tempted and vexed with many tribulations, yet "I will fear no evil" (Ps. 23:4), so long as Thy grace is with me. This alone and of itself is my strength; this alone brings counsel and help. This is stronger than all enemies, and wiser than all the company of the wise. Thy grace is the mistress of truth, the teacher of discipline, the light of the heart, the solace of affliction, the driver-away of sorrow, the expeller of fear, the nurse of devotion, the source and fountain of tears. Without this, what am I but a withered piece of wood, and an unprofitable branch only meet to be cast away (John 15:6)!

Let Thy grace therefore, O Lord, always both precede and follow me, and make me to be continually given to good works, through Jesus Christ Thy Son. Amen.

Chapter 56

DENY SELF AND IMITATE CHRIST

My son, the more you can go out of yourself, the more will you be able to enter into Me. Even to desire nothing that is without produces inward peace, so the forsaking of yourself inwardly joins you to God.

I wish you to learn perfect renunciation of yourself in My will, without contradiction or complaint.

Follow thou Me: "I am the way, the truth and the life" (John 14:6).

Without the Way, there is no going; without the Truth, there is no knowing; without the Life, there is no living. I am the Way, which you ought to follow; the Truth, which you ought to believe; the Life, which you ought to hope for. I am the Way inviolable, the Truth infallible, the Life unending. I am the Way that is straightest, the Truth that is highest, the Life that is truest, the Life blessed, the Life uncreated. If you remain in My way: "Ye shall know the truth and the truth shall make you free" (John 8:31, 32), and you shall lay hold on eternal life.

"If thou wilt enter into life, keep the commandments" (Matt. 19:17). If you will know the truth, believe Me. "If thou wilt be perfect, go and sell that thou hast" (John 19:21). If you will be My disciple, deny yourself utterly (Luke 9:23). If you will possess a blessed life, despise this present life. If you will be exalted in Heaven, humble yourself in this world (John 12:25). If you will reign with Me, bear the cross with Me (Luke 14:27). For only the servants of the cross find the way of blessedness and of true light.

O Lord Jesus, forasmuch as Thy way was narrow and despised by the world, grant me grace to imitate Thee, though with the world's contempt. "The disciple is not above his Master, nor the servant above his lord" (Matt. 10:24).

Let Thy servant be exercised in Thy life, for therein is my salvation and true holiness. Whatever I read or hear besides it does not refresh me nor delight me to the full.

My son, inasmuch as you know and have read all these things, happy shall you be, if you do them (John 13:17). "He that hath my commandments, and keepeth them, he it is that loveth me . . . and I will love him, and will manifest myself to him" (John 14:21), and will make him "sit with me in my throne" (Rev. 3:21).

O Lord Jesus, as Thou hast said and promised, so truly let it be, and let it be mine to win it. I have received the cross, I have received it from Thy hand. I will bear it, and bear it even unto death, as Thou hast laid it upon me. Truly a good man's life is the cross, but it guides him to Heaven. We have now begun; it is not lawful to go back, neither must we leave it.

Come, brethren, we go forward together; Jesus will be with us. For the sake of Jesus we have received this cross; for the sake of Jesus let us persevere in the cross. He will be our Helper, who is also our Guide and Forerunner. Behold, our King enters in before us, and He will fight for us. Let us follow manfully, let no man fear any terrors. Let us be ready to die valiantly in battle, nor bring such disgrace on our glory as to flee from the cross.

Chapter 57

WHEN MAN FALLS

MY SON, patience and humility in adversities are more pleasing to Me, than much comfort and devotion when things go well.

Why does a little matter spoken against you make you sad? Although it had been much more, you ought not to have been moved. But now let it pass. It is not the first that has happened, nor is it anything new; neither shall it be the last, if you live long.

You are manly enough, so long as nothing adverse befalls you. You can give good counsel also, and can strengthen others with your words; but when sudden tribulation comes to your door, you fail in counsel and in strength. Observe then your frailty, of which you too often have experience in small events. Notwithstanding it is done for your good, when these and such like trials happen to you.

Put it out of your heart according to your better knowledge, and if it has touched you, let it not cast you down, nor long perplex you. Bear it at least patiently, if you cannot joyfully. Although you are unwilling to hear it, and conceive indignation thereat, yet restrain yourself, and suffer no ill-ordered word to pass out of your mouth, whereby little ones may be offended. The storm which is now raised shall quickly be at peace, and inward grief shall be sweetened by the return of grace. I yet live, saith the Lord, and am ready to help you (Isa. 49), and to give you more than ordinary consolation, if you put your trust in Me, and call devoutly upon Me.

Be of more even mind, and gird yourself to greater endurance. All is not lost, although you feel yourself very often afflicted or grievously tempted. You are a man, and not God; you are flesh, not an angel. How could you continue always in the same state of virtue, when an angel in Heaven has failed in this, as also the first man in the Garden of Eden (Gen. 3)? I am He who lifts up the mourners to safety and soundness, and those who know their own weakness I advance to My own divine nature.

O Lord, blessed be Thy Word: "sweeter also than honey and the honeycomb" (Ps. 19:10; 119:103). What would I do in these great tribulations and straits, unless Thou didst comfort me with Thy holy discourses? What matter is it, what or how much I suffer if I may at length attain to the haven of safety?

210

Grant me a good end, grant me a happy passage out of this world. Remember me, O my God, and direct me in the right way to Thy kingdom.

Chapter 58

GOD'S SECRET JUDGMENTS

M Y SON, dispute not of high matters, nor of the secret judgments of God, why this man is so left, and that man taken into such great favor; why also one is so grievously afflicted, and another so eminently exalted. These things go beyond all reach of man's power, neither does any reason or disputation avail to search out the judgments of God.

When therefore the Enemy suggests these things, or some curious persons raise the question, let your answer be that of the psalmist: "Righteous art thou, O Lord, and upright are thy judgments" (Ps. 119:137). And again: "The judgments of the Lord are true and righteous altogether" (Ps. 19:9). My judgments are to be feared, not to be discussed; for they are not to be comprehended by the understanding of man.

If men would content themselves they would refrain from their vain discourses. They glory not of their own merits, inasmuch as they ascribe no goodness to themselves, but all to Me, since of My infinite love I have given them all things. They are filled with so great

211

love of the divine nature, and with such an overflowing joy, that no glory is wanting unto them, nor can they want aught of happiness. All the saints, the higher they are in glory, so much the humbler are they in themselves, and the nearer and dearer to Me. And therefore it is written, that they "cast their crowns before the throne, saying, Thou art worthy, O Lord, to receive glory and honor and power" (Rev. 4:10, 11).

Many inquire, who is the greatest in the kingdom of God, who know not whether they shall be meet to be numbered among the least. It is a great thing to be even the least in Heaven, where all are great; for they all shall be called, and shall be "the sons of God" (I John 3:1). "A little one shall become a thousand" (Isa. 60:22), "but the sinner being a hundred years old shall be accursed" (Isa. 65:20). For when the disciples asked who should be greatest in the kingdom of Heaven, they heard such an answer as this: "Except ye be converted, and become as little children, ye shall not enter into the kingdom of heaven. Whosoever therefore shall humble himself as this little child, the same is greatest in the kingdom of heaven" (Matt. 18:3).

Woe be unto them who disdain to humble themselves willingly with little children; because the low gate of the heavenly kingdom will not give them entrance (Matt. 7:14). Woe also to the rich, who have their consolations (Luke 6:24); for while the poor enter into the kingdom of God, they shall stand lamenting without.

212

Rejoice ye humble (Matt. 5:3), and be glad ye poor, for yours is the kingdom of God, if at least ye walk in the truth (II John 4).

Chapter 59

HOPE AND TRUST IN GOD ALONE

LORD, what is my confidence which I have in this life? Or what is my greatest comfort out of all things that are seen under Heaven? Is it not Thou, O Lord, my God, of whose mercies there is no number? Where has it ever been well with me without Thee? Or when could it be ill with me, when Thou wert present? I had rather be poor for Thee, than rich without Thee. I rather choose to be a pilgrim on earth with Thee, than without Thee to possess Heaven. Where Thou art, there is Heaven; and where Thou art not, there is death and Hell. Thou art all my desire, and therefore after Thee I sigh and call and earnestly pray. In short there is none whom I can fully trust in, none who can more seasonably help me in my necessities, but only Thou, my God. Thou art my hope, Thou my confidence; Thou art my Comforter, and in all things most faithful.

"All seek their own" (Phil. 2:21). Thou settest forward my salvation and my profit only, and turnest all things to my good. Although Thou exposest me to divers temptations and adversities, yet Thou orderest all this to my advantage, who art wont to try Thy beloved ones a thousand ways. In which trial of me Thou oughtest no less to be loved and praised, than if Thou wert filling me full of heavenly consolations. In Thee therefore, O Lord God, I place my whole hope and refuge; on Thee I rest all my tribulation and anguish; for I find all to be weak and inconstant, whatever I behold out of Thee.

For many friends will not profit, nor will strong helpers be able to assist, nor prudent counselors give a profitable answer, nor the books of the learned afford comfort, nor any precious substance deliver, nor any place, however retired and lovely, give shelter, unless Thou Thyself dost stand by, help, strengthen, console, instruct, and guard us. For without Thee all things that seem to belong to the possession of peace and bliss are nothing, and bring in truth no blessedness at all. Thou therefore art the perfection of all that is good, the height of life, the depth of all that can be spoken; and to hope in Thee above all things is the strongest comfort of Thy servants. To Thee therefore I lift up my eyes; in Thee my God, the Father of mercies, I put my trust.

Bless and sanctify my soul with Thy heavenly blessing, that it may become Thy holy habitation, and the seat of Thine eternal glory; and let nothing be found in this temple of Thy dignity, which shall offend the eyes of Thy majesty. According to the greatness of Thy goodness and multitude of Thy mercies look upon me (Ps. 51:2), and hear the prayer of Thy poor servant, who is far exiled from Thee "in the land of the shadow of death" (Isa. 9:2). Protect and keep the soul of me the meanest of Thy servants, amid so many dangers of this corruptible life, and by Thy grace accompanying me direct it along the way of peace to its native land of everlasting brightness.

Priest is the title given ordained ministers in certain churches, but the term applies also to him who has the title of pastor or minister because he is a person concerned with the services of the house of God; he performs the ceremonies of the church and is ready to explain the doctrines of his church. He is concerned also with the care of his people, particularly with their spiritual welfare.

Aaron and his sons were priests of Jehovah, as related in Exodus. Jesus Christ is called the High Priest of those who accept Him (Heb. 4:14, and other passages). In Revelation 1:6 and 5:10 we read that Jesus Christ has made us after our acceptance of Him, "kings and priests unto God and his Father."

—THE PUBLISHERS

The Fourth Book

A DEVOUT EXHORTATION TO THE HOLY COMMUNION

A DEVOUT EXHORTATION TO THE HOLY COMMUNION

The Voice of Christ.

"Come unto me, all ye that labor and are heavy-laden, and I will give you rest" (Matt. 11:28).

"The bread that I will give is my flesh . . . for the life of the world" (John 6:51).

"Take, eat: this is my body which is broken for you: this do in remembrance of me" (I Cor. 11:24).

"He that eateth my flesh, and drinketh my blood, dwelleth in me, and I in him" (John 6:56).

"The words that I speak unto you, are spirit, and they are life" (John 6:63).

Chapter 1

THE EMBLEMS OF CHRIST RECEIVED WITH REVERENCE

The Voice of the Disciple.

THESE ARE THY WORDS, O Christ the eternal truth, though not uttered all at one time, nor written together in one place. Because therefore they are Thine and true, they are all thankfully and faithfully to be received by me. Thine they are, and Thou hast uttered them; and they are mine also, because Thou hast spoken them for my salvation. I cheerfully receive them from Thy lips, that they may be deeply implanted in my heart. They stir me, those words of such tenderness, so full of sweetness and of love. But my own offenses make me afraid, and an impure conscience drives me back from receiving such great mysteries. The sweetness of Thy words invites me, but the multitude of my sins weighs me down.

Thou commandest me to come confidently unto Thee, if I would have part with Thee; and to receive the food of immortality, if I desire to obtain everlasting life and glory. "Come unto me [sayest Thou], all ye that labor and are heavy-laden, and I will give you rest." O sweet and loving word in the ear of a sinner, that Thou, my Lord God, shouldest invite the poor and needy to the communion of Thy most holy body!

But who am I, Lord, that I should presume to approach unto Thee? Behold, the "heaven of heavens cannot contain thee" and Thou sayest, "Come unto me." What does this most tender condescension and so loving an invitation mean? How shall I dare to come, who know not any good in myself, whereupon I may presume? How shall I bring Thee into my house, I who have so often offended Thy most gracious countenance? Angels and archangels stand in awe of Thee, holy and righteous men fear Thee, and sayest Thou, "Come unto me"? Unless Thou, O Lord, didst say this, who would believe it to be true? And unless Thou didst command it, who could attempt to draw near?

Behold Noah, that just man labored a hundred years in the making of the ark, that he might be saved with a few; and how can I in one hour's time prepare myself to commune with the Maker of the world?

Moses, Thy great servant, and Thy special friend, made an Ark of incorruptible wood, which he clothed with the finest gold, that therein he might lay up the Tables of the Law (Exod. 25:10-16), and I, a corrupted creature, shall I dare so lightly to entertain Thee the Maker of the Law, and the Giver of life?

Solomon the wisest of the kings of Israel bestowed seven years in building a Temple to the praise of Thy name (I Kings 6:38); for eight days he celebrated the feas' of dedication thereof. He offered a thousand peace-offerings, and the Ark of the Covenant he solemnly set in the place prepared for it, with the sound of trumpets and great joy (I Kings 8). And I the most miserable and poorest of men, how shall I receive Thee into my house, I who scarcely know how to spend one-half hour in true devotion? And I would that I could even spend one-half hour worthily!

O my God, how earnestly they studied to please Thee! Alas, how little I do! How short a time I spend, when I am preparing myself to receive the communion! Seldom am I wholly collected; very seldom am I cleansed from all distraction. And yet surely in the presence of Thy Godhead no unbecoming thought ought to intrude itself, nor should any creature occupy my heart; for it is not an angel, but the Lord of the angels, whom I am about to entertain as my Guest.

However, very great is the difference between the Ark of the Covenant with its contents, and Thy most pure body with its unspeakable virtues. Great is the difference between those legal sacrifices, figures of things to come, and the true sacrifice of Thy body, the fulfillment of all ancient sacrifices. Wherefore then am I not more on fire to seek Thy adorable presence? Why do I not prepare myself with greater solicitude to receive the sacred emblems? Whereas those holy patriarchs and prophets of old, kings also and princes, with the whole people, showed such zeal of devotion to Thy divine service.

The most devout king David danced before the Ark of God with all his might, calling to mind the benefits bestowed in time past upon his forefathers. He made instruments of various kinds; he set forth psalms, and appointed them to be chanted with joy; he himself played on the harp, being inspired with the grace of God. He taught the people of Israel to praise God with their whole hearts, and with the voice of melody to bless and praise Him every day.

If so great devotion was then used, and such divine praise was kept up before the Ark of the Testament, what reverence and devotion ought now to be preserved by me and all Christian people, in the presence of this sacrament of Thy holy communion!

O God, the invisible Creator of the world, how wonderfully Thou dost deal with us; how sweetly and graciously Thou dost order all things for Thine elect! This verily passes all understanding; this specially draws the hearts of the devout, and kindles their affection. For even thy true faithful ones, who spend their whole lives in reformation oftentimes gain much grace of devotion and love of virtue by partaking of the communion.

Our lukewarmness and negligence are exceedingly to be lamented and pitied, that we are not drawn with greater affection to Christ; in whom lies all the hope of those that are to be saved. For He Himself is our "sanctification, and redemption" (I Cor. 1:30). He is the consolation of pilgrims, and the everlasting fruition of saints. It is therefore to be lamented that many so little consider this divine mystery.

Thanks be unto Thee, Lord Jesus, eternal Shepherd, that Thou hast vouchsafed to refresh us, who are poor and exiles, with Thy precious body and blood; and to invite us to partake in these mysteries by a message even from Thine own lips, saying: "Come unto me, all ye that labor and are heavy-laden, and I will give you rest."

Chapter 2

GOODNESS AND LOVE OF GOD EXHIBITED IN THIS SACRAMENT

The Voice of the Disciple.

IN CONFIDENCE of Thy goodness and great mercy, O Lord, I draw near, sick to the Healer, hungry and thirsty to the Fountain of life, needy to the King of Heaven, a servant to his Lord, a creature to the Creator, desolate to my own tender Comforter.

What am I, that Thou shouldest grant me Thine own self. How dare a sinner appear before Thee? And how is it that Thou dost vouchsafe to come to a sinner? Thou knowest Thy servant, and art well aware that he has in him no good thing, for which Thou shouldest grant him this.

I confess therefore my own vileness, I acknowledge Thy goodness, I praise Thy tender mercy, and give Thee thanks for Thy transcendent love. For Thou doest this for Thine own sake, not for any merits of mine; to the end that Thy goodness may be the better known unto me, Thy love more abundantly heaped upon me, and Thy humility more eminently set forth.

Since therefore this is Thy pleasure, and Thou hast commanded that it should be so, this Thy condescension is also pleasing unto me. Oh, that my iniquity may not bar the way!

O most sweet and most tender Jesus, how great reverence and thanksgiving, together with perpetual praise, is due unto Thee for the sacrifice of Thy sacred body; whose worthiness no one among men is found able to express! But on what shall I think at this communion, in approaching my Lord, whom I am not able duly to honor, and yet whom I desire devoutly to apprehend? What can I think on better, and more profitable, than to humble myself before Thee, and to exalt above myself Thy infinite goodness? I praise Thee, my God, and exalt Thee forever. I despise myself and cast myself down before Thee, into the depths of my own vileness.

Behold, Thou art the Holy of holies, and I the lowest of sinners! Behold, Thou inclinest Thyself unto me, who am not worthy to look up unto Thee! Behold, Thou comest unto me; it is Thy will to be with me, Thou invitest me to Thy banquet. Thou art willing to give me heavenly food and bread of angels to eat which is indeed no other than the living Bread, "which cometh down from heaven, and giveth life unto the world" (Ps. 78:25; John 6:33).

Behold, from whence love proceeds! What condescension shines forth! How great thanks and praises are due unto Thee for these benefits! Oh, how salutary and profitable was Thy counsel, when Thou didst ordain it! How sweet and pleasant the banquet, when

Thou gavest Thyself to be our food! Oh, how admirable is Thy working! O Lord, how mighty is Thy power, how unspeakable Thy truth! For Thou didst speak and all things were made (Gen. 1; Ps. 148:5); and this was done which Thou didst command. A wondrous thing, worthy of faith, and surpassing man's understanding, that Thou, my Lord God, true God and Man, art represented under the form of a little bread and wine, which are eaten by him who receives them.

Thou who art the Lord of the universe, and standest in need of none (Ps. 16:2), art pleased to dwell in us. Do Thou preserve my heart and body undefiled, that with a cheerful and pure conscience I may be able very frequently to celebrate Thy mysteries, and to receive to my everlasting health, those things which Thou didst consecrate and ordain for Thine own special honor and for a never-ceasing memorial.

Rejoice, O my soul, and give thanks to God, for so noble a gift, and so marvelous a consolation, left to you in this vale of tears. For as often as you repeat this mystery, and receive this spiritual nourishment, so often you go over the work of your redemption, and are reminded of all the merits of Christ. For the love of Christ is never diminished, and the greatness of His propitiation is never exhausted.

Therefore you ought ever to prepare yourself hereunto by a fresh renewing of your mind, and to weigh with attentive thought the great mystery of salvation. So great, so new, and so joyful ought it to seem to you, when you partake of this sacrament, as if on this same day Christ first descending into the womb of the Virgin became Man, or hanging on the cross this day suffered and died for the salvation of mankind.

Chapter 3

PROFITABLE TO COMMUNICATE OFTEN

The Voice of the Disciple.

BEHOLD, O LORD, I come unto Thee, that it may be well with me through Thy gift, and that I may rejoice in Thy holy feast, which Thou, O God, "hast prepared of thy goodness for the poor" (Ps. 68:10). Behold, in Thee is all that I can or ought to desire; Thou art my salvation and my redemption, my hope and my strength, my honor and glory.

"Rejoice the soul of thy servant: for unto thee, O Lord, do I lift up my soul" (Ps. 86:4). I long to appropriate Thee now with devotion and reverence. I desire to bring Thee into my house, that with Zacchaeus I may be counted worthy to be blessed by Thee, and to be numbered among the sons of Abraham (Luke 19:9). My soul desires to receive Thee; my heart longs to be united with Thee. Give Thyself to me, and it will suffice; for beside Thee no comfort avails.

Without Thee I cannot be, and without Thy visitation I have no power to live. And therefore I must often draw near unto Thee, and obtain from Thee the medicine of my salvation; lest I faint in the way, if I be deprived of the heavenly nourishment. For so, most merciful Jesus, Thou once didst say, preaching to the people and curing divers sicknesses: "I will not send them away fasting, lest they faint in the way" (Matt. 15:32; Mark 8:8). Deal Thou therefore in like manner now with me.

It is indeed necessary for me, who so often fall and sin, so quickly wax dull and faint, that by frequent prayer and confession, and receiving Thy grace in this ordinance, I renew, cleanse and kindle myself, lest by too long abstaining I fall away from my holy purpose. "For the imagination of man's heart is evil from his youth" (Gen. 8:21); and unless some divine remedy help him, he by and by falls away to worse things. Holy communion therefore draws us back from evil, and makes us strong in good. For if I am now so often negligent and lukewarm when I communicate, what would become of me if I sought not after such great help? And although I may not be fit, I will endeavor notwithstanding at due times to receive the divine mysteries, and to offer myself as partaker of such great grace. For this is the one chief consolation of the faithful soul, so long as it is absent from Thee in this mortal body, that being mindful of its God, it should often commune with its Beloved, with devout mind.

Oh, the wonderful condescension of Thy tender mercy toward us, that Thou, O Lord God, the Creator and Life-giver of all spirits, dost vouchsafe to come

227

unto the soul of the poor, and with Thy whole Godhead and manhood abundantly to satisfy its famishing hunger!

Thou my sweetest, most Beloved! Let Heaven and earth and all their fair apparel be silent before Thy face; for what praise and beauty they have, it is received from Thy bounteous condescension, nor shall they ever attain unto the beauty of Thy name, whose "understanding is infinite" (Ps. 147:5).

Chapter 4

BENEFITS BESTOWED

The Voice of the Disciple.

O LORD, MY GOD, do Thou grant unto Thy servant "the blessings of goodness" (Ps. 21:3), that I may be enabled to approach worthily and devoutly to Thy glorious sacrament.

Stir up my heart toward Thee, and set me free from heavy listlessness. "Visit me with thy salvation" (Ps. 106:4), that I may taste in spirit Thy sweetness, which lies hidden in this sacrament as in a fountain.

Enlighten also my eyes to behold so great a mystery, and strengthen me with undoubting faith to believe it. For it is Thy work, and no human power; Thy sacred institution, not man's invention. For of himself no man is found able to comprehend and understand these things, which pass even the subtilty of angels. What portion then of so deep a mystery shall I, unworthy sinner, dust and ashes, be able to search out and comprehend? O Lord, in the simplicity of my heart, with a good and firm faith, and at Thy commandment, I draw near unto Thee with hope and reverence.

For Thou hast bestowed, and still oftentimes dost bestow, many benefits in this sacrament upon Thy beloved ones who communicate devoutly, O my God, the Upholder of my soul, the Restorer of human weakness, and the Giver of all inward consolation. For Thou impartest unto them much comfort against every variety of tribulation, and liftest them up from the depth of their own dejected state, to hope in Thy protection; and dost inwardly recreate and enlighten them with a new grace, so that they who at first and before communion felt themselves full of anxiety and without affection, afterward, being refreshed with heavenly meat and drink, do find themselves changed for the better.

And in such a way of dispensation as this dealest Thou with Thine elect, in order that they may truly acknowledge, and clearly prove, how great is their infirmity, and what goodness and grace they obtain from Thee. For they of themselves are cold, hard, and undevout; but by Thee they are enabled to become fervent, cheerful, and devout.

For who is there, that approaching humbly unto a fountain of sweetness, does not carry away some little sweetness? Or who, standing near a great fire, receives not some small heat therefrom? And Thou art a fountain always full and overflowing; a fire ever burning and never going out (Isa. 12:3; Lev. 6:13). Wherefore if I am not permitted to draw out of the fullness of the fountain, nor to drink my fill, I will notwithstanding set my lips to the mouth of this heavenly conduit, that I may receive from thence at least some small drop to refresh my thirst, and may not wither. And though I cannot as yet be altogether heavenly, nor so on fire as the cherubim and seraphim, yet notwithstanding I will endeavor to apply myself earnestly to devotion, and to prepare my heart to obtain but some small flame of divine fire.

But whatever is wanting in me, O Jesus, most holy Saviour, do Thou in my behalf bountifully and graciously supply, Thou who hast vouchsafed to call us all unto Thee, saying: "Come unto me, all ye that labor and are heavy-laden, and I will give you rest." I indeed labor in the sweat of my brow (Gen. 3:19). I am racked with grief of heart, I am burdened with sins, I am troubled with temptations, I am entangled and oppressed with many evil passions; and there is none to help me, none to deliver and save me, but Thou, O Lord God my Saviour, to whom I commit myself and all that is mine, that Thou mayest keep watch over me, and bring me safe to life everlasting. Receive me for the honor and glory of Thy name, Thou who hast given Thy body and blood to be my meat and drink. Grant, O Lord God of my salvation, that by frequenting Thy mysteries, the zeal of my devotion may increase.

Chapter 5

DIGNITY OF THE SACRAMENT
AND PRIESTLY WORK

The Voice of the Beloved.

THE PRIEST IS INDEED the minister of God, using the Word of God, by God's command and appointment. Nevertheless God is there the principal Author and invisible Worker; to whom all that He wills is subject, and all that He commands is obedient (Gen. 1; Ps. 49:7; Rom. 9:20).

"Take heed unto thyself" (I Tim. 4:16), and see what that is, whereof the ministry has been delivered to you by the laying on of the bishop's hand.

Behold, you have been made a priest; see now that you perform your office faithfully and devoutly, and show yourself without reproof. You have not lightened your burden, but are now bound with a straiter band of discipline, and are obliged to a more perfect degree of sanctity. A priest ought to be adorned with all virtues, and to give example of good life to others. His conversation (Phil. 3:20) is not in the vulgar and common ways of mankind, but with the angels in Heaven, or with perfect men on earth.

A priest is Christ's ambassador, that with all supplication and humility he may beseech God for himself and for the whole people (Heb. 5:3). He has both before and behind him the sign of the Lord's cross, for the continual bringing to mind of the passion of Christ. He bears the cross that he may diligently look on Christ's footsteps, and earnestly study to follow them. He is signed with the cross, that he may cheerfully endure, for God's sake, any evils inflicted on him by others. He bears the cross, that he may mourn for his own sins; and that he may with sympathy and tears lament for the faults of others also, and know that he has been placed in the midst between God and the sinner (Ps. 106:23). Neither ought he to grow slack in prayer and holy oblation, till he prevail to obtain grace and mercy.

When a priest celebrates his office faithfully, he honors God.

Chapter 6

SPIRITUAL EXERCISE BEFORE COMMUNION

The Voice of the Disciple.

WHEN I WEIGH Thy worthiness, O Lord, and my own vileness, I exceedingly tremble, and am confounded within myself. For if I do not draw near, I flee from life; and if I unworthily intrude myself, I incur Thy displeasure. What therefore shall I do, O my God, my Helper and my Counselor in necessities?

Teach Thou me the right way; appoint me some brief exercise suitable for holy communion. For it is good for me to know how with devotion and reverence I should prepare my heart for Thee.

Chapter 7

SEARCHING OUR OWN CONSCIENCE

The Voice of the Beloved.

DILIGENTLY EXAMINE your conscience, and to the utmost of your power purify and make it clear, with true contrition and humble confession; so you may have no burden, nor know anything that may breed remorse of conscience, and hinder your drawing near. Think with displeasure of all your sins in general, and more particularly bewail and lament your daily transgressions. And if time permits, confess to God in the secret of your heart all the wretchedness of your evil passions. Groan and lament that you are yet so carnal and worldly, so unmortified from passions; so full of the motions of concupiscence, so unwatchful over your outward senses, so often entangled with many vain imaginations. So much inclined to outward things, so negligent in things inward. So lightly moved to laughter and unbridled mirth, so hardly to tears and contrition. So swift to ease and pleasures of the flesh, so dull to zeal and strictness of life. So curious to hear what is new, and to see what is beautiful, so slack to embrace what is humble and mean. So covetous of abundance, so niggardly in giving, so close in keeping. So inconsiderate in speech, so reluctant to keep silence. So unruly in manners, so fretful in conduct. So eager about food, so deaf to the Word of God. So swift to take rest, so slow to labor. So wakeful after gossiping tales, so drowsy at the sacred services of the night; so hasty to arrive at the end, so inclined to wandering and inattention. So careless in observing the hours of prayer, so lukewarm in celebrating, so dry in communicating. So quickly distracted, so seldom thoroughly self-collected. So suddenly moved to anger, so apt to take displeasure against another. So ready to judge, so severe to reprove. So joyful at prosperity, so weak in adversity. So often making many good resolutions, and yet bringing them at last to so poor effect.

These and other defects being confessed and bewailed with sorrow and great displeasure at your own infirmity, make a firm resolution to be always amending your life, and making progress in all that is good.

Then, with full resignation and with your entire will, offer up yourself to the honor of My name, on the altar of your heart a perpetual whole burnt offering, even your body and soul, faithfully committing them unto Me.

Chapter 8

THE SACRIFICE OF CHRIST ON THE CROSS, AND RESIGNATION OF OURSELVES

The Voice of the Beloved.

As I of My own will offered up Myself unto God the Father for your sins (Isa. 53:5; Heb. 9:28), My hands stretched out on the cross, and My body stripped bare, so that nothing remained in Me that was not wholly turned into a sacrifice of divine propitiation, in like manner you ought also to offer yourself willingly to Me every day, as a pure and sacred offering, with all your powers and affections, unto the utmost strength of your soul.

What do I require more than that you study to resign yourself entirely to Me? Whatever you give besides yourself, I regard not; for I seek not your gift, but you (Prov. 23:26). As it would not satisfy you to have all things without Me; so neither can it please Me, whatever you give, if you offer not yourself. Offer up yourself to Me, and give yourself wholly for God, and your offering shall be accepted. Behold, I offered up Myself wholly unto My Father for you. I gave also My whole body and blood for you, that I might be wholly yours, and that you might continue to be Mine to the end. But if you stand upon yourself, and do not offer yourself up freely to My will, the offering is not complete, neither will there be entire union between us.

Therefore a free-will offering of yourself into the hands of God ought to go before all your works, if you desire to obtain liberty and grace. For this is why so few become illuminated and inwardly free, because they do not wholly deny themselves.

My sentence stands sure: "Whosoever he be of you that forsaketh not all, he cannot be my disciple" (Luke 14:33). If you therefore desire to be My disciple, offer up yourself to Me with all your affections.

Chapter 9

OFFERING OURSELVES WHOLLY TO GOD

The Voice of the Disciple.

THINE, O LORD, are all things that are in Heaven, and that are in earth (Ps. 24:1). I desire to offer up myself unto Thee, as a free-will offering, and to continue Thine forever. O Lord, in the simplicity of my heart I offer myself unto Thee this day to be Thy servant forever, in humble submission, and for a sacrifice of perpetual praise.

Lord, I offer unto Thee, on Thy propitiatory altar,

all my sins and offenses, which I have committed before Thee and Thy holy angels, from the day wherein I first could sin even to this hour; that Thou mayest consume and burn them, one and all, with the fire of Thy love, and blot out all the stains of my sins, and cleanse my conscience from every offense, and restore to me Thy grace which by sinning I lost, fully forgiving me all, and admitting me mercifully to the kiss of peace.

What can I do but humbly confess and bewail my sins (Ps. 32:5), and unceasingly entreat Thy propitiation? I entreat Thee, hear me with Thy favor, when I stand before Thee my God. All my sins are exceedingly displeasing to me. For them I grieve, and will grieve as long as I live, being ready to practice repentance, and to the utmost of my power to make restitution. Forgive me, O God, forgive me my sins for the sake of Thy holy name. Save Thou my soul, which Thou hast redeemed with Thy precious blood. Behold, I commit myself unto Thy mercy, I resign myself into Thy hands. Deal with me according to Thy goodness, not according to my wickedness and iniquity.

I offer up also unto Thee all that is good in me, though it be very small and imperfect, in order that Thou mayest amend and sanctify it; that Thou mayest make it grateful and acceptable unto Thee, and always be perfecting it more and more; and bring me also, a slothful and unprofitable wretch, to a blessed and worthy end.

Moreover I offer up unto Thee all the pious desires

of devout persons, the necessities of parents, friends, brethren, sisters, and of all who are dear to me, and of those who have done good to myself or to others for Thy love; and who have desired and sought of me to offer prayers for themselves and for all that are theirs, that all may feel the present help of Thy grace, the aid of Thy consolation, protection from dangers, deliverance from punishment; and that being rescued from all evils, they may with joy return worthy thanksgivings unto Thee.

I offer up also unto Thee my prayers and sacrifices of propitiation, for those especially who have in any matter hurt, grieved, or reviled me, or who have done me any damage or displeasure. For all those also, whom at any time I have grieved, troubled, burdened, and scandalized, by words or deeds, knowingly or in ignorance; that Thou wouldst grant us all equally pardon for our sins, and for our offenses against each other.

Take away from our hearts, O Lord, all suspicion, indignation, wrath, and contention, and whatever may wound and lessen brotherly love.

Have mercy, O Lord, have mercy on those who crave Thy mercy, give grace unto them that stand in need thereof, and make us such that we may be worthy to enjoy to the full Thy grace, and go forward to life eternal.

Chapter 10

COMMUNION NOT TO BE TAKEN LIGHTLY

The Voice of the Beloved.

YOU OUGHT to often go back to the Fountain of grace and divine mercy, to the Fountain of goodness and of all purity.

The Enemy, knowing the exceeding great profit and healing which lies in the holy communion, endeavors by every means and occasion to the utmost of his power to withdraw and hinder faithful and devout persons from partaking therein. Some persons suffer the worst insinuations of Satan, when they are preparing to fit themselves for holy communion. For that wicked spirit himself comes among the sons of God (Job 1:6) to trouble them according to his accustomed malice, or to render them overly fearful and perplexed, that he may diminish their affection, or by his assaults take away their faith; to the end they may altogether forbear communicating, or come with lukewarmness.

But take no heed at all of his wiles and phantoms, but all his vain imaginations are to be turned back upon his own head. You must despise and laugh to scorn the wretched one, nor on account of his assaults,

239

or for the troubles which he raises, omit the holy communion.

Oftentimes also an overly great solicitude for the obtaining of devotion, and some anxiety or other about the confession of sins, hinders them. Act according to the counsel of the wise (Prov. 13:1), and lay aside anxiety and scrupulousness; for it hinders the grace of God, and overthrows the devotion of the mind.

Do not omit the holy communion for every small vexation and trouble, but rather proceed at once to confess your sins, and cheerfully forgive others all their offenses (Matt. 5:24). And if you have offended any, humbly crave pardon, and God will readily forgive you.

How happy is he and how acceptable to God, who so lives, and in such purity guards his conscience, that he is prepared and well-disposed to communicate even every day, if it were in his power, and he might do it without others taking notice!

If a person sometimes abstains out of humility, or by reason of some lawful cause preventing him, he is to be commended for his reverence. But if a drowsiness have crept over him, he must stir up himself, and do what lies in him, and the Lord will assist his desire, because of his good will, which is what God chiefly regards. But when he is lawfully hindered he will yet always have a good will, and a pious intention to communicate. For it is in the power of any devout person every day and every hour profitably and without hindrance to draw near to the spiritual communion of Christ. And yet on certain days, and at times appointed, he ought to observe sacramentally, with affectionate reverence, and rather seek the honor and glory of God, than his own comfort (I Cor. 11:23-26). For he communicates mystically, and is invisibly refreshed, as often as he devoutly calls to mind the mystery of the Incarnation and the passion of Christ, and is inflamed with the love of Him.

Blessed is he who offers up himself as a whole burnt offering to the Lord, as often as he communicates.

Be not too slow nor too quick in celebrating, but keep the good accustomed manner of those with whom you live. You ought not to cause trouble and weariness to others, but to keep the accustomed path, according to the appointment of our Fathers; and rather be a servant to the edification of others, than to your own devotion or affection.

Chapter 11

THE BLOOD OF CHRIST AND THE HOLY SCRIPTURES NECESSARY

The Voice of the Disciple.

O LORD JESUS, how great is the pleasure of the devout soul that feasts with Thee in Thy banquet; where there is set no other food to be eaten but Thyself; the only Beloved, and most to be desired above all the desires of the heart! To me also it would be indeed sweet, in Thy presence to pour forth tears from the bottom of my heart, and with the grateful Magdalene to wash Thy feet with tears (Luke 7:38). But where is that devotion? Where that plenteous flowing of tears?

While I think on these wonders, even all spiritual comfort becomes heavy and wearisome to me; because as long as I behold not my Lord openly in His own glory, I account as nothing all that I see and hear in this world. Nothing can comfort me, no creature can give me rest, but only Thou my God, whom I earnestly desire to contemplate everlastingly. But this is not possible, so long as I linger in this mortal life. Therefore I must frame myself to much patience; and submit myself to Thee in every desire. For even Thy saints, O Lord, who now rejoice with Thee in the kingdom of Heaven, while they lived, waited in faith and in great patience for the coming of Thy glory (Heb. 10:35, 36; 11:39, 40). What they believed, I believe; what they hoped, I hope; where they are, by Thy grace I trust I shall come. In the meantime, I will walk in faith, strengthened by the examples of the saints. I have also books for my comfort and for the looking glass of my life; and above all these, I have Thy presence for a singular remedy and refuge.

Two things I perceive to be exceedingly necessary for me in this life; without which this miserable life would be intolerable to me. While I am detained in the prison of this body, I acknowledge myself to stand in need of food and light. Thou hast given therefore unto me in my weakness Thy sacred companionship, for the refreshment of soul and body (John 6:51); and Thou hast set as "a lamp unto my feet" (Ps. 119:105) Thy Word. Without these two I should not be able to live; for the Word of God is the light of my soul, and Thyself the Bread of life. These also may be called the two tables, set on this side and on that, in the treasure-house of the Church (Ps. 23:5; Heb. 9:2-4; 13:10). One table is that of the precious blood of Christ. The other is that óf the divine Law, containing holy doctrine; teaching men the right faith, and steadfastly leading them onward even to the things "within the vail" (Heb. 9:19), where is the Holy of holies.

Thanks be unto Thee, O Lord Jesus, Thou Light of everlasting Light, for that table of sacred doctrine, which Thou hast prepared for us by Thy servants the prophets and apostles and other teachers. Thanks be unto Thee, O Thou Creator and Redeemer of mankind, who, to manifest Thy love to the whole world, hast prepared a great supper, wherein Thou hast set before us to be eaten, not the typical lamb, but the emblems of Thine own most sacred body and blood (John 6:53-56); making glad all the faithful with this sacred banquet.

Oh, how clean those hands ought to be, how pure the lips, how holy the body, how unspotted the heart of the priest, to whom the Author of purity so often draws near! From the lips of the priest, nothing but what is holy, no word but what is good and profitable ought to proceed. Single and chaste ought to be his eyes that are wont to serve the Church, the body of

Christ; the hands should be pure and lifted up to Heaven. Unto the priests more especially it is said in the Law: "Ye shall be holy: for I the Lord your God am holy" (Lev. 19:2; 20:26; I Peter 1:16).

Assist us with Thy grace, Almighty God, that we who have undertaken the office of the priesthood may be able to wait on Thee worthily and devoutly, in all purity, and with a good conscience. And if we cannot dwell in as great innocency of life as we ought, grant to us at least worthily to lament the ills which we have committed; and in the spirit of humility, and with the full purpose of a good will, to serve Thee more earnestly for the time to come.

Chapter 12

PREPARE WITH GREAT DILIGENCE

The Voice of the Beloved.

I AM THE LOVER OF PURITY and the Giver of all holiness. I seek a pure heart, and there is the place of my rest (Ps. 24:4; Matt. 5:8). "Make ready for us . . . a large upper room furnished . . . where I shall eat the passover with my disciples" (Mark 14:14, 15; Luke 22:11, 12). If you will have Me come to you, and remain with you, "purge out . . . the old leaven" (I Cor. 5:7), and make clean the habitation of your heart. Shut out the whole world, and all your sins; sit as it were "a sparrow alone upon the housetop" (Ps. 102:7), and think over your transgressions in the bitterness of your soul. For everyone that loves prepares the best and fairest place for his beloved; for herein is known the affection of him who entertains his beloved.

Know, notwithstanding, that no merit of any action of yours is able to make this preparation sufficient, although you prepare yourself a whole year together, and have nothing else in mind. But it is out of My mere goodness and favor that you are permitted to approach My table; as if a beggar were invited to a rich man's table, and he has no other return to make to him for his benefits, but to humble himself and give him thanks.

When I bestow on you the grace of devotion, give thanks to your God; not because you are worthy, but because I have had mercy on you.

You ought however not only to prepare yourself to devotion before communion, but also carefully to preserve yourself therein, after you have received the sacrament. Nor is the careful guard of yourself afterward less required than devout preparation before. For a good guard afterward is the best preparation again for the obtaining of greater grace. For if one gives himself up at once to too much outward consolations, he is rendered thereby exceedingly indisposed to devotion.

Beware of much talk (Prov. 10:19), remain in some secret place, and enjoy your God; for you have Him, whom all the world cannot take from you. I am He, to whom you ought wholly to give up yourself, that you may now live no longer in yourself, but in Me, free from all anxiety of mind.

Chapter 13

SEEK UNION WITH CHRIST IN THE SACRAMENT

The Voice of the Disciple.

WHO WILL GRANT unto me, Lord, to find Thee alone (Song of Sol. 8:1), and to open unto Thee my whole heart, and enjoy Thee even as my soul desires; and that henceforth none may look upon me, nor any creature move me, nor have regard to me; but that Thou alone mayest speak to me; and I to Thee, as the beloved is wont to speak to his beloved, and friend to feast with friend (Exod. 33:11).

This I long for, that I may be wholly united unto Thee, and may withdraw my heart from all created things, and by means of sacred communion, and the frequent partaking thereof, may learn more and more to relish things heavenly and eternal. Ah, Lord God, when shall I be wholly made one with Thee, and lost in Thee, and become altogether forgetful of myself? Thou in me, and I in Thee (John 15:4); so also grant that we may both continue together in one. Verily, Thou art "my beloved . . . the chiefest among ten thousand" (Song of Sol. 5:10), in whom my soul is well pleased to dwell all the days of her life. Verily, Thou art my Peacemaker, in whom is highest peace and true rest; out of whom is labor and sorrow and infinite misery. "Verily, thou art a God that hidest thyself" (Isa. 45:15), and Thy counsel is not with the wicked, but with the humble and "he giveth grace unto the lowly" (Prov. 3:34).

Surely there is no other nation so great, that hath gods so nigh unto them, as Thou our God art present to all Thy faithful ones, unto whom for their daily comfort, and for the raising up of their hearts to Heaven, Thou bestowest Thyself to be appropriated and enjoyed. For what other nation is there of such high renown, as the Christian people (Deut. 4:7, 8)? Or what creature under Heaven is there so beloved, as the devout soul into which God Himself enters?

O unspeakable grace! O wondrous condescension! O unmeasurable love bestowed on man!

But what return shall I make to the Lord for this grace (Ps. 116:12), for love so unparalleled? There is nothing else that I am able to present more acceptable, than to offer my heart wholly to my God, and to unite it most inwardly unto Him.

Then shall all my inward parts rejoice, when my soul shall be perfectly made one with God. Then will He say unto me: "If thou art willing to be with Me, I am willing to be with thee." And I will answer Him: "Vouchsafe, O Lord, to remain with me, I will gladly be with Thee. This is my whole desire, that my heart be made one with Thee."

Chapter 14

THE DESIRE OF THE DEVOUT

The Voice of the Disciple.

OH, HOW GREAT is thy goodness, which thou hast laid up for them that fear thee!" (Ps. 31:19).

When I call to mind some devout persons, who approach Thy sacrament, O Lord, with the greatest devotion and affection, I am oftentimes confounded and blush within myself, that I come with such lukewarmness, yea coldness, to the table of sacred communion. I remain so dry, and without affection of heart; I am not wholly set on fire in Thy presence, O my God, nor so earnestly drawn and affected as many devout persons have been, who out of a vehement desire of the communion, and a heart-felt love, were unable to restrain themselves from weeping.

Oh, the truly burning faith of those, standing forth as a probable evidence of Thy sacred presence! For they truly know their Lord "in breaking of bread" (Luke 24:32-35), whose heart within them so vehemently burns, while Thou, O blessed Jesus, dost walk with them.

Far from me often is such affection and devotion, such vehement love and fervency.

Be thou favorable unto me, O Jesus, most gracious Lord, and grant to me Thy poor and needy creature, sometimes at least, in this holy communion to feel a little of the heart-felt passion of Thy love; that my faith may become stronger, my hope in Thy goodness may go forward, and that love once perfectly kindled within me, after the tasting of this heavenly manna, may never decay.

Thy mercy however is able to grant me even the grace which I long for, and, in the day of Thy good pleasure, to visit me most graciously with the Spirit of fervor. For although I burn not with so great desire as theirs who are so especially devoted unto Thee, yet notwithstanding, by Thy grace, I have a desire for this great and burning desire, praying and longing that I may have my part with all such Thy fervent lovers, and be numbered in their holy company.

Chapter 15

THE GRACE OF DEVOTION

The Voice of the Beloved.

YOU OUGHT EARNESTLY to seek the grace of devotion, fervently to ask for it, patiently and with confidence to wait for it, gratefully to receive it, humbly to keep it, diligently to work with it. And to commit to God the term and manner of the heavenly visitation until it come to you.

You ought especially to humble yourself, when you feel inwardly little or no devotion; but not to be too much cast down, nor to grieve inordinately. God often gives in one short moment, that which He for a long time denied. He gives sometimes in the end, that which in the beginning of your prayer He deferred to give. If grace were always presently given, and were at hand even with a wish, weak man could not well bear it. Therefore the grace of devotion is to be waited for, with good hope and humble patience.

Nevertheless, to yourself, and to your own sins impute it when this grace is not given you, or when it is secretly taken away. It is sometimes but a small matter that hinders and hides grace; at least if anything can be called small, and not rather a weighty matter, which keeps away such great good. And if you remove this, be it great or small, and perfectly overcome it, you will have your desire. For immediately, as soon as you give yourself to God from your whole heart, and seek neither this nor that, according to your own liking or will, but settle yourself wholly in Him, you shall find yourself united and at peace. For nothing can have so sweet a savor, nothing please so well, as the good pleasure of the divine will.

Whosoever therefore, with a single heart lifts up his attention to God, and empties himself of all inordinate love or dislike of any created thing, he shall be the fittest to receive grace, and meet for the gift of true devotion. For the Lord bestows His blessings there, where He finds the vessels empty. And the more perfectly one forsakes these low things, and the more he by contempt of himself dies to himself, so much the more speedily grace comes, the more plentifully it enters in, and the higher it lifts up the free heart.

"Then shalt thou see, and flow together, and thine heart shall fear" (Isa. 60:5) within, because the hand of the Lord is with you, and you have put yourself wholly into His hand, even forever and ever. "Behold . . . thus shall the man be blessed" (Ps. 128:4), who seeks God with his whole heart (Ps. 119:2), and "lifteth not up his soul unto vanity" (Ps. 24:4). This man in going to holy communion obtains the great grace of divine union; because it is not to his own devotion and comfort that he has regard, but above all devotion and comfort to the honor and glory of God.

Chapter 16

MAKE KNOWN OUR NEEDS TO CHRIST

The Voice of the Disciple.

O THOU MOST LOVING LORD, whom now with all devotion I desire to receive, Thou knowest mine infirmity and the necessity which I endure; my great evils and sins; how often I am weighed down, tempted, disturbed, and defiled. I speak to Thee who knowest all things, to whom all my inward thoughts are open, and who alone canst perfectly comfort and help me. Thou knowest what good things I stand in most need of, and how poor I am in virtues. Behold, I stand before Thee poor and naked, calling for grace and imploring mercy.

Refresh Thy hungry beggar, inflame my coldness with the fire of Thy love, enlighten my blindness with the brightness of Thy presence. Turn for me all earthly things into bitterness, all things grievous and contrary into patience, all low and created things into contempt and oblivion. Lift up my heart to Thee in Heaven, and send me not away to wander over the earth (Gen. 4:12-14). Be Thou alone sweet to me, from henceforth forevermore. Thou alone art my meat and drink, my love and my joy, my sweetness and all my good.

Oh, that with Thy presence Thou wouldest wholly inflame, consume, and transform me into Thyself; that I might be made one Spirit with Thee (I Cor. 6:17), by the grace of inward union, and by the meltings of ardent love! Suffer me not to go away from Thee hungry and dry, but deal mercifully with me, as oftentimes Thou hast dealt wonderfully with Thy saints. What marvel is it if I should be wholly on fire from Thee, and of myself fail and come to nothing; since Thou art Fire always burning and never failing, Love purifying the heart, and enlightening the understanding!

Chapter 17

UNITED WITH CHRIST

The Voice of the Disciple.

I DESIRE to appropriate Thee with the most vehement desire, and the most worthy reverence, that any of the saints ever had, or was able to feel. And although I be unworthy to possess all those feelings of devotion, nevertheless I·offer unto Thee the whole affection of my heart, as if I alone had all those most grateful and burning longings after Thee. Yea, and all that a holy soul can conceive and desire, I do, with the deepest reverence and most inward fervor, offer and present unto Thee. I desire to reserve nothing unto myself, but freely and most cheerfully to sacrifice unto Thee myself and all that is mine.

O Lord my God, my Creator and my Redeemer, I desire to appropriate Thee this day, with such affection, reverence, praise, and honor, with such gratitude, worthiness and love, with such faith, hope, and purity, as Thy most holy mother, the Virgin Mary, desired Thee with, when to the angel who declared unto her glad tidings of the mystery of the Incarnation, she humbly and devoutly answered: "Behold the handmaid of the Lord; be it unto me according to thy word" (Luke 1:38). And as Thy forerunner, John the

Baptist, rejoicing in Thy presence, leaped for joy of the Holy Spirit, while he was yet shut up in his mother's womb (Luke 1:44). And afterward seeing Jesus walking among men, he humbled himself exceedingly, and said with devout affection: "The friend of the bridegroom, which standeth and heareth him, rejoiceth greatly because of the bridegroom's voice" (John 3:29). In like manner do I also wish to be on fire with great and holy desires, and to offer myself up to Thee from my whole heart. Wherefore also for myself, and for all such as are commended to me in prayer, I offer and present unto Thee the triumphant joys, the burning affections, and inward ecstasies, the supernatural illuminations and celestial visions of all devout hearts, with all the virtues and praises celebrated, and to be celebrated by all creatures in Heaven and in earth; that by all Thou mayest worthily be praised and glorified forever.

Receive, O Lord my God, my wishes and desires of giving Thee infinite praise, and blessing that has no bounds, which according to the measure of Thine ineffable greatness, are unto Thee most justly due. These I render to Thee, and long to render every day and every moment. And with prayers and zeal I invite and beseech all heavenly spirits, and all Thy faithful servants, to render with me thanks and praises unto Thee. Let all people, nations, and languages praise Thee (Ps. 117), and magnify Thy holy name with exultation and burning devotion.

Chapter 18

HUMILITY AND FAITH IN THE HOLY SACRAMENT PRESCRIBED

The Voice of the Beloved.

YOU OUGHT TO BEWARE of curious and unprofitable searching into this most profound sacrament, if you will not be plunged into the depths of doubt. "For men to search their own glory is not glory" (Prov. 25:27). God is able to work more than man can understand. A loving and humble inquiry after the truth is permitted, if it be ready to be taught, and studied to walk according to the sound precepts of the Fathers. It is a blessed simplicity which leaves the difficult ways of questionings, and goes forward in the plain and firm path of God's commandments.

Many have lost devotion, while they sought to search into things too high. Faith is required and a sincere life; not height of understanding, nor the depths of the mysteries of God. If you do not understand, nor grasp the things that are beneath you, how shall you comprehend those which are above you (John 3)? Submit yourself unto God, and humble your sense to faith; and the light of knowledge shall be given you, in such degree as shall be profitable and necessary.

Some are grievously tempted, but this is not to be imputed to themselves, but rather to the Enemy. Be not anxious; dispute not with your own thoughts, nor give any answer to doubts suggested by the Devil. But trust the words of God, trust His saints and prophets, and the wicked Enemy will flee.

Oftentimes it is very profitable that the servant of God endure such things. For the Devil tempts not unbelievers and sinners, whom he already has in his possession; but he tempts and disquiets the faithful and devout in various ways.

God deceives not; he is deceived who trusts too much to himself. God walks with the simple (Ps. 19:7; 119:130; Matt. 11:25), reveals Himself to the humble, gives understanding to the little ones, opens the sense to pure minds, and hides grace from the curious and proud. Human reason is feeble and may be deceived, but true faith cannot be deceived.

All reason and natural searching ought to follow faith, not to go before it, nor to break in upon it. For faith and love here have the pre-eminence, and work in hidden ways, in this holy sacrament. God, who is eternal, and incomprehensible, and of infinite power, does things great and unsearchable in Heaven and in earth, and there is no tracing out of His marvelous works. If the works of God were such that they might be easily comprehended by human reason, they could not be justly called marvelous or unspeakable.